COOKING WITH MY FRIENDS

Cooking With My Friends

Kentucky Recipes, Tried and True

LaVece Hughes

Wind Publications
2003

First Edition

International Standard Book Number   1-893239-16-0
Library of Congress Control Number   2002116413

Also by LaVece Hughes, *A Dickinson Heritage Cookbook* (1993)

Front cover – Pineapple Meringue, page 147

Foreword

Few of the recipes that we use are truly our own. Most are gifts—the most treasured being those we receive from friends penciled on crumpled pieces of napkin, or 3 x 5 cards, dog-eared and grease-stained. Others we have gleaned from favorite books, newspaper columns or magazines, and carried in our pockets or purses until nearly illegible before having the opportunity to add them to our kitchen files. We gratefully accept these gifts, enhance them with our own special touches and embellishments, and pass them on as our own as gifts to those we love, or whose friendship we value.

There is much enjoyment in tracing the genealogy of our favorite recipes. *This recipe comes from my friend, Sandy, the associate principal at Happydale High, who grew up in Central City just down the road from my home town of Glasgow . . .* Just as we like to know our own origins, it is interesting to know the origin and lineage of our recipes—we are comforted in the knowledge that the recipes we use have had a continuing value in the provision of sustenance and are considered worthy of being passed on.

Many of the recipes in this book are adapted from an earlier book of my family's recipes, *Generations: A Dickinson Heritage Cookbook.* The years since the publication of *Generations* has seen the growing popularity of quicker and easier recipes. Many of today's favorite recipes use mixes or other timesaving devices and ingredients in their preparation. *Cooking With My Friends* reflects this trend toward speed and convenience. However, quality has not been sacrificed for speed and convenience. Many of the recipes included here are those oldies, time-tested and proven to be the best.

I come from a large family, and I remember from childhood that meal preparation was often begun with the question, "What's for dessert?" And for the rest of the meal, "Now, what else will we have?" My family was known to sit often for long discussions over dessert, and therefore Mother considered desserts very important, and probably the most challenging and enjoyable aspect of cooking. I believe their preparation was a way in which she chose to express her artistic inclinations. The Dickinson family's Pineapple Meringue and Pumpkin Pie is the stuff of legend. In spite of this sweet approach to meal preparation, proper nutrition was always emphasized. The question which initiated Mother's meal preparation in those days, and which I still ask today, explains the emphasis on dessert recipes in this book.

So it is with heartfelt appreciation and gratitude for my friends and family that I now pass on these recipes, precious to me, as gifts to my family, friends, and the readers of this book.

Contents

Appetizers

Breakfast

Breads

Salads

Fruits & Vegetables

Meat

Pies

Cakes

Cookies

Drinks

Candies

Appetizers

Apple Dip
Mary McMurray

8 oz cream cheese, softened
1 c powdered sugar
caramel dip (commercial)

chopped cashews
Gala or favorite apples—cored
  and sliced

Mix cream cheese and powdered sugar and pour into a Tupperware bowl, lined with saran wrap. Chill. Turn out on plate and place caramel dip on top. Add cashews. Serve with apple slices.

Apple Caramel . . . you can make it yourself
Pat Nickell

Immerse an unopened can of Eagle Brand Milk in a pan of water. Bring to a boil and reduce heat to low. Cook on low for and hour and turn off heat. Cool. When ready to serve open and pour into serving dish. Serve with Granny Smith Apple slices.

Hot Artichoke Dip
LaVece Hughes

1 can (14 oz) artichoke hearts,
  drained, chopped
1 c (4 oz) grated Parmesan cheese
1 c Miracle Whip

1 clove garlic
minced chopped tomatoes
sliced green onions

Mix all ingredients except tomatoes and onions. Spoon into a 9-inch pie plate. Bake at 350 degrees for 20 or 25 minutes or until lightly browned. Sprinkle with tomato and onions, it desired. Serve with Triscuits. Can be made ahead.

> *"If change is to come, it will come from the margins. It was the desert, not the temple, that gave us the prophets."*
> — *Wendell Berry*

Bacon Cheese Ring
LaVece Hughes

12 oz bacon, cooked and crumbled
1 lb sharp cheddar cheese, grated
1 t red pepper
1 bunch green onions, finely chopped

2 cups mayonnaise
1 pkg slivered almonds, toasted
strawberry preserves
Breton crackers

Spray a salad ring with Pam. Place toasted almonds in the bottom. Mix remaining ingredients except strawberry preserves and crackers and press into the mold. Refrigerate overnight. Serve with strawberry preserves and Breton Crackers.

Beer Cheese
Deanna Smith

2 lb Velveeta cheese at room temp
12 oz Hellmann's mayonnaise
4½ oz Durkee's red hot sauce

8 oz beer (room temp)
¼ c dried onion flakes
¼ t Garlic powder

Mix well.
This is difficult because you can't melt the Velveeta. I usually cut/break the Velveeta into small chunks, add the mayo and use my electric mixer to start the process. Then I gradually add everything else and alternate between stirring and the mixer until I have everything mixed well.

Bacon Tomato Dip
Stan Mitchell

1 c mayonnaise
1 c sour cream

1 lb bacon crumbled
1 tomato, diced

Mix and serve with your favorite crackers.

"Best dip ever. Tastes like a BTL."

> *"I am not offended by the dumb blonde jokes. I know that*
> *I am not dumb, and I know that I'm not blonde."*
> — *Dolly Parton*

Dried Beef Cheese Ball
Ora Lee Henry

2 8-oz pkg cream cheese
1 pkg dried chopped beef
1 T mayonnaise

1 T yellow mustard
2 T Lipton Onion soup mix

Cream together and shape into a ball; Make ahead and let set in refrigerator at least over night. *I usually serve with Rye Crackers.*

Creamy Broccoli Dip
LaVece Hughes

8 oz light cream cheese
2 T milk
1 c finely chopped cooked
    broccoli

2 T Gray Poupon Dijon mustard
¼ c chopped green pepper

Mix and chill. Serve with Chicken In a Basket Crackers.

Cheese Krispies
Latie Ross from Mattie Menaugh

2 c grated sharp cheddar
2 sticks margarine
2 c flour
¼ t pepper

½ t salt
2 c Rice Krispies
pecan halves, optional

Blend cheese and margarine well, then add rest of ingredients except pecans. Chill; roll into balls; flatten with fork; top each with a pecan half if desired. Bake at 375 degrees for 10 minutes. Make six dozen.

Privacy is one those thing that we take for granted until it has been violated. – Monica Lowenski

Cheese Olive Balls

LaVece Hughes

1 c freshly grated sharp
    cheese (less 2 T)
3 T soft butter
¼ t salt

½ c sifted flour
½ t paprika
24 stuffed olives

Form ball by putting small amount of cheese mixture around an olive.
Bake on a cookie tin or un-greased pan at 400 degrees for 10-15 minutes.

Crabmeat Munchie . . . quick and easy

LaVece Hughes

1 can of crab meat
1 8-oz pkg cream cheese

1 bottle cocktail sauce
crackers

Soften cream cheese and spread on a large plate. Pour cocktail sauce to
near the edge of the cream cheese. Open a can of crabmeat and place the
crab on the cocktail sauce. Serve with crackers.

This can be made just before serving

Curried Cream Cheese Ball . . . really good

Melinda Watt

2 8-oz cream cheese
2 T butter
3 T curry

1 lb bacon
Raffetto brand chutney
Club or Townhouse crackers

Blend cream cheese in food processor. Add butter and curry powder.
Line a bowl with Saran Wrap and form cheese mixture into to a ball
Refrigerate several hours. Fry bacon and crumble. Put cheese ball on
platter and smother with chutney, then bacon. Serve with crackers.
Replenish chutney and bacon.

The first rule of love is to listen.

Egg Plant Dip
Sharon Perry

1 egg plant, peeled and cut in 1-inch cubes
1 red Bell pepper, chopped
1 T tomato paste
1 red onion, chopped
1 T olive oil
3 garlic cloves, crushed

Bake at 350 degrees for 1 hr on a greased cookie sheet. (Add crushed garlic near end of baking) Blend eggplant with 1 T olive oil and tomato paste until well blended. Salt and pepper to taste. Serve with toasted Pita bread.

Fruit Cheese Ball . . . great
Kim Overstreet

2 8-oz pkg cream cheese
1 small vanilla instant pudding
1 can fruit cocktail, drained
toffee Heath Bits (found in chocolate chip section)
lemon snaps or ginger snaps

Mix cream cheese and pudding. Fold in fruit cocktail. Roll in Heath Bits and serve with lemon snaps or ginger snaps.

Fruit Dip . . . marvelous
Linda Eldridge

1 small instant vanilla pudding
1¼ c milk
1 small frozen orange juice
¼ c sour cream

Mix and beat pudding, milk, and orange juice for two minutes. Add sour cream and chill. Serve with small pieces of your favorite fruits.

Did you know? A cigarette costs ¼ of a cent to manufacture, or 5 cents to produce an entire pack. Somebody is making a big profit.

Mini-Ham Squares
LaVece Hughes

1 2½-oz pkg processed ham, chopped
1 small onion, chopped
½ c shredded Swiss Cheese
1½ t Dijon mustard
⅛ t pepper
1 tube refrigerated crescent rolls
1 egg, beaten

Preheat oven to 350 degrees. Dice ham and onion. In bowl combine and mix with cheese, egg, pepper and mustard. Spread crescent roll dough on baking pan, pinching seams to seal. Spread ham mixture on crust and bake about 20 minutes. Cut in small squares for serving.

Mexican Dip
LaVece Hughes

1 can bean dip
1 ripe avocado, mashed
½ pkg dry taco mix
½ c mayonnaise
½ c sour cream
2 tomatoes
5 green onions
1 can black olives
1 small pkg shredded cheddar cheese

Layer in this order:
Spread bean dip on serving plate, add mashed avocado. Mix taco mix, mayonnaise and sour cream and spread on top of avocado. Chop tomatoes and green onions. Pour on top of sour cream mixtures. Layer olives on top, then cheese. Chill and serve with tortilla chips.

Cheese Nips
Peggy Worms

2⅔ c flour
1 lb sharp cheddar cheese
2 sticks butter

Blend with mixer. Refrigerate for several hours if possible. Work with hands into narrow rolls and freeze; Slice and place on a cookie sheet, and cook at 300 degrees for 30 minutes.

When opening canned goods, open the end that had been sitting on the shelf. The ingredients come out more easily, and that end is usually cleaner.

Microwave Caramel Corn . . . crunchy
LaVece Hughes

4 quarts popped corn	¼ c corn syrup
1 c brown sugar	½ t salt
¾ stick butter or margarine	½ t soda

Place one brown paper grocery bag inside another. Put popped corn into the doubled grocery bag. Combine brown sugar, margarine, syrup and salt in a 2-quart deep bowl. Bring to a boil in the microwave (about 4 minutes); then cook on high for 2 minutes. Remove from microwave and stir in baking powder. Mix well and immediately pour syrup over popped corn. Close bag by turning the top down and shake to mix and coat corn. Cook bag in microwave for 1½ minutes. Remove from microwave and *SHAKE, BABY SHAKE!* Repeat this cooking-shaking process for 2 more times. Pour out onto wax paper, spread, cool, and break apart. Store in closed container.

We usually double this. It is great, easy and quick. Our family has even made this during the half time of a TV basketball game.

Olive Dip
Betty Mulberry

1 8-oz pkg cream cheese	16 oz chopped stuffed olives
1 c Hellmann's mayonnaise	1½ c chopped pecans
(no substitutes)	½ c of olive juice (more if necessary)
¼ t white pepper	

Mix well and serve with your favorite crackers.

Reuben Dip
Ellen Dennison

1 c mayonnaise	1 small onion chopped
16 oz sauerkraut (well drained)	2 c shredded Swiss cheese
4 2½-oz jars Armour dried beef	

Drain the sauerkraut between paper towels, and chop up the dried beef. Mix well. Cook for 30 minutes at 350 degrees. Serve with Triscuit Crackers.

Party Mix
Selma Dickinson and LaVece Hughes

1 box Rice Check
1 box thin pretzels
1 box Wheat Check
1 box Cheerios
4 c peanuts
1 T Worcestershire sauce

1 T garlic salt
1 T Seasoned Salt
1 t Tabasco
1 heaping t curry powder
2 c oil (or less)

Mix oil, salts and sauces. Place cereals, pretzels, and nuts in big pans with deep sides. Pour oil mixture over all, gently stir and bake for 2 hours at 200 degrees. Store in tight container. Favorite cereals may be substituted.

This is a family favorite. I make it in massive quantities to give and eat at Christmas. Aunt Selma used melted butter, but the oil makes it less greasy. -- lgh

Party Pinwheels
Rebecca McKinney from Bea Hall

2 8-oz pkg cream cheese
1 pkg Original Milk Recipe
   Hidden Valley Ranch
   dressing mix
2 green onions, chopped

½ c diced pimentos or red peppers
½ c celery, diced
1 can (2 oz or more) diced
   black or green olives
4 10-inch tortillas

Mix all ingredients except tortillas and spread mixture on the flour tortillas. Roll each one up tight and chill. Slice each roll.

Sausage Balls
Lib Cannon

1 lb sausage
1 10-oz pkg shredded cheese

3½ c Bisquick

Combine all ingredients with hands. Shape into small balls and bake 350 degrees for 15-20 minutes. Can be made ahead and frozen in an airtight container.

Spinach Dip
Elizabeth Brents Dickinson

10-oz pkg frozen chopped spinach
1 c mayonnaise
1 c sour cream

1 medium onion, chopped
8 oz can water chestnuts, drained
⅝-oz pkg vegetable soup mix

Thaw spinach; place on paper towel and press until barely moist. Combine spinach, mayonnaise, sour cream, onion water chestnuts, and vegetable soup mix. Stir well. Cover and chill several hours before serving with favorite crackers.

Vegetable Dip
LaVece Hughes

1 cup mayonnaise
½ c chopped fresh parsley
1 T grated onion
¼ t salt
⅛ t curry powder

½ cup whipping cream, whipped
2 T minced fresh chives
1-½ t lemon juice
¼ t paprika
1 small clove garlic, minced

Combine all ingredients; stir well. Chill 3 hours. Serve with fresh vegetables.

Chili/Cheddar Dip . . . simple
LaVece Hughes

2 8-oz pkg cream cheese, softened
15 oz chili without beans
16 oz shredded cheddar cheese

Spread cream cheese on bottom of Pyrex dish. Spread a layer of chili over cream cheese. Finish with a layer of shredded Cheddar cheese. Microwave for 5 minutes or until cheese melts. Serve with tortilla chips.

Attitude
By Charles Swindoll

The longer I live, the more I realize the impact of attitude on life. Attitude, to me, is more important than facts. It is more important than education, than money, than circumstances, than failures, than successes, than what other people think or say or do. It is more important than appearance, giftedness or skills. It will make or break a company . . . a church . . . a home. The remarkable thing is we have a choice every day regarding the attitude we will embrace for that day. We cannot change our past . . . we cannot change the fact that people will act in a certain way. We cannot change the inevitable. The only thing we can do is play on the one string we have, and that is our attitude . . . I am convinced that life is 10% what happens to me and 90% how I react to it. And so it is with you . . . we are in charge of our attitudes.

Breakfast

Baked Apple Pancake

LaVece Hughes

1 c pancake mix
⅔ c milk
2 T oil
1 egg, beaten

¼ c margarine
⅓ c packed brown sugar
2 medium apples, peeled and sliced
maple syrup

Combine pancake mix, milk, oil and egg in a large mixing bowl. Melt butter in an 8-inch skillet. Mix in brown sugar and apple slices; sauté until sugar is dissolved. Pour batter over apple mixture. Cook, uncovered, over medium heat until bubbles form on top of pancake. Bake in oven at 350 degrees for 15-20 minutes or until golden brown. Invert on a serving platter. Serve with syrup.

Beer Muffins

Anne Karsner

4 c Bisquick
2 t sugar
1 12-oz can beer

Mix all ingredients, beat vigorously for 30 seconds. Fill hot greased muffin tins ⅔ full. Bake for 15 minutes at 400 degrees.

French Toast

Kate Ganter

2 eggs
¼ c sugar
½ t cinnamon

½ c milk
4 or 5 slices bread

Beat eggs, then beat in the sugar and then the milk and cinnamon. Soak the bread slices in mixture and fry in a skillet with margarine.

"An eye for an eye will make the world go blind."
— Mohamdas K. Ghandi

Sausage Biscuits
Frieda Walters

1 lb sausage
2 ⅔ c flour
2 T sugar
1 t baking powder
1 c buttermilk
Melted butter

½ t salt
½ t soda
½ c shortening
1 pkg dry yeast
¼ c very warm water

Fry crumbled sausage till done. Drain. Sift dry ingredients. Cut in shortening: Dissolve yeast in warm water for 5 minutes. Add yeast to buttermilk. Stir in dry ingredients. Either pat or roll to ¼ in thick, brush with melted butter. Sprinkle sausage over ½ of dough. Fold over. Cut into squares. Place on cookie sheet and freeze. Remove and store in plastic bag in freezer until ready to use. Take only what is needed and bake frozen for 10-12 minutes at 450 degrees.

"These are absolutely fantastic and can be made at a moment's notice!"

Blueberry Nut Bread
LaVece Hughes

1 pt blueberries, rinsed but
    not dried
3 c plus 3 T flour, divided
2 c sugar
1 c chopped nuts

1 c oil
4 eggs
1 t baking soda
1 t ground cinnamon
1 t salt

Preheat the oven to 350 degrees and coat two 9 x 5 loaf pans with Pam. In a medium bowl, combine the damp blueberries and 3 T flour; toss to coat evenly. In a large bowl, combine the remaining ingredients and mix well. Carefully stir in the coated blueberries, and then spoon the mixture into two loaf pans. Bake 55-60 minutes or until a wooden tooth pick inserted in the center comes out clean. Allow to cool slightly, and then remove to a wire rack to cool completely. Serve with cream cheese.

Housework is something you do that nobody notices....
Unless you don't do it!

Stuffed French Toast
LaVece Hughes

8 slices sourdough bread
2 bananas
½ c sugar
1 t cinnamon

2 eggs
½ c milk
1 t vanilla

Cut bananas lengthwise, and then crosswise to get about 8 pieces flat on one side. Cut pockets in each piece of bread, insert a banana slice in each. Mix sugar and cinnamon and set aside. Mix eggs, milk and vanilla in shallow dish. Soak sandwiches, turning once, about 6 minutes. Heat oil in large saucepan or skillet to 350 degrees. Add sandwiches, sauté until golden brown, place on paper towels and sprinkle with cinnamon sugar.

Garlic Omelet
Martha Dickinson

2 T oil
2 eggs
1 T water

1 T yogurt (nonfat, low fat or regular
1 T parsley or cilantro, chopped
1 clove garlic

optional: 1 tablespoon of grated cheddar cheese and/or salsa

Crush or chop 1 clove of garlic and add to folded eggs with 1 T water and a pinch of salt and pepper. Heat olive oil in skillet. Pour eggs gently into skillet. When the eggs solidify a bit, add the rest of the ingredients to the center and fold the omelet in half and cook until its just right. *Please don't overcook.* Serve with a sprig of parsley on the side.

Do something every day to make other people happy,
Even it it's just to leave them alone.

I always knew that I wanted to grow up and be somebody, but I
realize now that I should have been more specific.
— Lily Tomlin

Oven Baked Eggs and Sausage
Mary Lou Dickinson

12 eggs, beaten
2 c milk
6 slices bread
1 t salt

1 c sharp or milk cheese, grated
1½ lb sausage (may *substitute*
      bacon or link sausage)
2 t Worcestershire sauce

Brown sausage and drain. Place bread in bottom of a greased 9 X 19 inch pan. Mix remainder and pour over bread. Allow to stand in refrigerator overnight. Put in cold oven and bake in a covered pan for 1 hour at 350 degrees.

Christmas Morning Egg Casserole
Georgia Dickinson Peterson

2 c seasoned croutons
1½ c shredded sharp
    cheddar cheese (6 oz)
6 eggs, beaten

½ t salt
½ t dry mustard
⅛ t pepper
2 c milk

Place croutons in a greased 10 x 6 x 2 baking dish. Sprinkle cheese over croutons. Combine remaining ingredients mix well. Pour egg mixture into casserole. Bake at 350 degrees for 25 minutes.

"May be made the day before".

Hard-Boiled Egg Casserole
Letha Sloan

12 eggs, boiled and halved
5 oz ham, chopped
buttered toast crumbs (3 slices)

Make 3 cups white sauce:
Melt 3 T butter, stir in 6 T flour over low heat. Slowly stir in 3 cups of milk. Add dash salt and pepper. Heat and stir until thickened.

Layer ham and egg halves in flat Pyrex dish. Pour white sauce over top. Cover with buttered breadcrumbs. Warm in oven before serving.

Girl Scout Eggs
LaVece Hughes

Cut circles out of the center of bread slices with a biscuit cutter. Heat a skillet with a little butter and toast the bread on one side. Turn toast over and fill the holes with eggs and cook until done. May also toast the small circles.

"This is a great way to get children to eat eggs and can be eaten with the hands."

Christmas Morning Cranberry Casserole ... yummy
Georgia Peterson and Lelia Ann Smith

3 c chopped apples
2 c fresh cranberries
2 T flour
1 c sugar
3 1⅝-oz pkg instant oatmeal
    with cinnamon

¾ c chopped pecans
½ c flour
½ c brown sugar
½ c margarine
* additional cranberries and
    pecans for topping

Combine apples, cranberries and flour, tossing to coat. Add 1 cup sugar, mixing well. Place in a 2 qt casserole dish. Combine oatmeal, chopped pecans, ½ c flour and brown sugar; add butter and stir well. Spoon over fruit mixture. Bake uncovered at 350 degree for 45 minutes. Garnish with cranberries and pecan pieces before baking.

Garden Bounty
LaVece Hughes

6 slices bacon
3 large potatoes, chopped and
    boiled
1-2 banana peppers, chopped

4 diced tomatoes, or 14-oz can
    with its juice
6 eggs
salt and pepper to taste

Cook bacon until crisp in large skillet. Remove from skillet. When cool, break into pieces. Add potatoes to grease in skillet. Add peppers, tomatoes, and bacon pieces. Beat eggs and pour on top of potato mixture. Cook 15 minutes on medium heat until heated through and eggs are done. Salt and pepper to taste.

Orange Breakfast Ring
LaVece Hughes

1 c sugar
3 T grated orange rind
2 12-oz cans biscuits
½ c margarine

3 oz cream cheese, softened
½ c powdered sugar
2 T orange juice

Combine sugar and orange rind. Separate biscuits; dip each in butter and coat with sugar mixture. Stand biscuits on edges in a 9-inch tube pan and bake at 350 degrees for 30 minutes or until brown. Invert on serving plate and remove ring from pan. Combine cream cheese and powdered sugar. Add juice, stirring well. Spoon over top of breakfast ring. Serve warm.

Sticky Buns
Leslie Bosse

24 frozen white dinner roll dough balls
1 small box (cook and serve)
    butterscotch pudding
½ c butter

¾ t cinnamon
¾ c brown sugar
½ c chopped nuts

Spray a Bundt pan well with Pam. Sprinkle nuts evenly in bottom of pan. Place frozen dough balls on top of nuts. Sprinkle dry pudding over dough balls. In small saucepan, melt butter. Add cinnamon and brown sugar and allow to simmer for five minutes. Pour over dough balls. Cover with a greased, light piece of foil and allow to sit overnight on counter to rise. Bake uncovered at 350 degrees for 15 minutes, then cover with foil (to prevent browning) and bake another 15 minutes. Let stand for 5 minutes and then invert.

"We make these on Christmas Eve to have for Christmas morning."

To remove glue from jars and new glassware, try rubbing the glue with white vinegar.

When in doubt...throw it out. If it looks or smells strange, just chuck it. Remember that cooked poultry dishes keep for 3 or 4 days only in the refrigerator, uncooked bacon lasts a week; fresh eggs three weeks.

Raspberry-Cheese Coffee Cake

LaVece Hughes

8 oz cream cheese, softened
½ c butter, softened
1 c sugar
2 large eggs
¼ c milk
½ t vanilla

1¾ cups flour
1 t baking powder
½ t baking soda
¼ t salt
½ cups raspberry preserves
3 T powdered sugar, for garnish

Beat first 3 ingredients at medium speed until creamy. Combine eggs, milk, and vanilla, beating until smooth. Add while mixing, flour and next 3 ingredients; to cream cheese mixture. Beat at slow speed until well blended. Pour batter into a greased and floured 9 x 13 pan. Dollop with preserves and swirl with a knife. Bake at 350 degrees for 30 minutes or until cake begins to shrink from sides of pan. Cool for a few moments, then sprinkle with powdered sugar. Cut into squares.

Lexington, Kentucky's new hockey team, The Men-O-War, were formerly in Macon, Georgia, where they were known as the Macon Whoopee . . .

"Injustice anywhere is a threat to justice everywhere."
— Martin Luther King, from the Birmingham Jail

Bread

Angel Biscuits
Mary Lynn Dickinson

1½ pkg quick-acting
   dry yeast
5 c self rising flour

¼ c sugar
1 c shortening or lard
2 c buttermilk

Stir flour, yeast and sugar together. Cut in lard until size of peas. Mix in buttermilk. *"I mix by hand, putting finger tips at top of each side, going down and lifting up until moist. Then fold in bottom sides to the middle. Just fold, DO NOT WORK."* Knead about 3 times and roll out ¼" thick, and cut with a 3" biscuit cutter. Fold in half and place on a lightly greased baking sheet. Brush with melted butter, and bake at 400 degrees for 15 to 20 minutes.

Apricot Oatmeal Muffins
Joan Walker

2 c buttermilk
1 c rolled oats
2 eggs
¾ c brown sugar
½ -1 c dried apricots, plumped *
   and chopped

1⅔ c whole-wheat flour
1 t baking soda
1 t cinnamon
1 t salt
2 T vegetable oil

Combine buttermilk and oats, stir; cover and refrigerate overnight. Preheat oven to 400 degrees. Line muffin tins with paper baking cups. Put eggs in bowl and beat just to blend. Add sugar and beat till smooth. Add buttermilk-oat mixture and mix. Combine dry ingredients and oil to above mixture and stir just until blended. Add apricots. Bake in muffin tins 15-20 minutes, till lightly browned.

Variations: Instead of apricots use raisins, chopped walnuts, or both.

* To plump dried fruit, soak in warm water.

Banana Bread from Aunt Lovie

Selma Goodman Dickinson

1 c sugar
½ c shortening
3 large bananas, mashed
2 eggs
2 c flour

½ c nuts
1 t soda in 2 T water
½ t salt
1 t vanilla

Cream sugar and shortening. Add eggs. Add remaining ingredients. Bake in a greased loaf pan at 375 degrees for 40 minutes.

Beaten Biscuits from Aunt Byrd Rogers

Lelia Rogers Dickinson

7 c flour
1 c lard
1 t salt

2 to 4 T sugar
1 t baking powder
1⅓ c cold milk

Sift dry ingredients together. Blend lard. Add milk. Work on beaten biscuit roller about twenty minutes or until dough is smooth and satiny and the blisters will pop. Roll to desired thickness. Cut with 1½ inch biscuit cutter. Place on baking sheet. Prick each biscuit three times with a fork, making sure it goes all the way through to the pan. Bake at 350 degrees for thirty to forty minutes. Makes about eighty small biscuits.

This old Southern recipe was made for special occasions to serve with country ham.

Stress is what happens when your gut says "No"
And your mouth says, "Of course, I'd be glad to."

Cheesy Chive Corn Bread
LaVece Hughes

1 c corn meal
¼ c sugar
2 eggs
¼ c melted butter
3 T minced chives

1 c flour
4 t baking powder
1 c milk
1 c shredded sharp cheese

Combine cornmeal, flour, sugar, and baking powder. In another bowl, whisk eggs, milk, butter. Stir into dry ingredients just until moistened. Fold in cheese and chives. Bake in 13 x 9 baking dish for 18 minutes at 400 degrees. Cut into strips and serve warm.

Hush Puppies
LaVece Hughes

1 c corn meal
½ c flour
1½ t soda
½ t salt
½ c sugar

1 egg
½ c buttermilk
1 or 2 medium onions, chopped
Oil for deep frying

Mix and sift dry ingredients. Add beaten egg, buttermilk and onion. Mix well. Drop by spoonfuls into oil. When cooked, drain on paper towel

Johnny Cake . . . an old southern favorite
LaVece Ganter Dickinson

¾ c sifted flour
1 t baking soda
½ t salt
1½ c yellow corn meal
2 T sugar

2 eggs, well beaten
¼ c white vinegar
1 c sweet milk
¼ c melted shortening

Sift flour with baking soda, salt and sugar. Stir in cornmeal. Combine eggs, vinegar, milk and shortening. Add to dry ingredients and stir until dry ingredients are just dampened. Turn into greased 8 x 8 x 2 pan. Bake for 30-35 minutes at 400 degrees.

"We used to eat Johnny Cake with green beans and tomatoes for lunch almost everyday in the summer," remembers daughter, Mary Lynn.

Orange Date Nut Bread
Billie Neal Howard Dickinson

1 large orange
1 c pitted dates
1 t soda
⅔ c sugar
2 T butter
1 t vanilla

1 beaten egg
2 c sifted flour
1 t baking powder
¼ t salt
½ c nuts

Squeeze juice from the orange into a cup measure. Add boiling water to make 1 cup liquid. Put orange rind through food chopper and add enough dates (chopped) to equal 1 cup. Place into mixing bowl. Add juice. Stir in soda, sugar, butter and vanilla. Add beaten egg, then flour which has been sifted with baking powder and salt. Add nuts. Place in pan greased with shortening and floured. Bake in pre-heated oven for 50 minutes at 350 degrees in 2 small or 1 long loaf pan. Cool. Slice thin and spread with cream cheese, crushed pineapple and flaked coconut mixed together.

Quick Muffins . . . easy baking
LaVece Ganter Dickinson

1 c self-rising flour
½ c milk
3 T mayonnaise

Mix all together and bake in a greased muffin tin at 425 degree

A friend is someone who understands your past, believes in your future,
And accepts you today just the way you are.   Proverbs 27:17

Pumpkin Bread
Lelia Ann Dickinson Smith, from Momma Jane Howard

2 c sugar
1 c oil
4 beaten eggs
1 16-oz can pumpkin
3½ c flour
2 t soda
⅔ c water

2 t salt
1 t baking powder
1 t nutmeg
1 t allspice
1 t cinnamon
½ t cloves
optional: coconut raisins, nuts

Combine and mix oil, eggs and pumpkin. Add and mix flour, soda, salt, baking powder, spices and water. Add raisins, coconut and nuts. Bake at 350 degrees for 1½ hours. Makes 2 loaves.

Spoon Bread . . . southern cornbread
LaVece Hughes

2 c corn meal
1 T sugar
1½ c buttermilk
1 t soda

2 t salt
1½ t butter
2 eggs

Scald corn meal with enough hot water to make consistency of mush. Add sugar, salt, and butter and cool. Beat eggs; dissolve soda in buttermilk and beat mixture all together. Place mixture in greased casserole and bake 30-40 minutes in hot oven. Serve by spoonfuls from dish.

Easy Spoon Bread
LaVece Hughes

1 stick butter
2 eggs
8-oz box of corn muffin mix

16 oz creamed corn
8 oz sour cream

Mix all ingredients and pour into a casserole dish. Bake at 350 degrees for 40 minutes. *Really good and really quick.*

Whole Wheat Bread from Maggie Jones

Selma Goodman Dickinson

Cream together:

1 c shortening (Crisco)	1 c water, lukewarm
¾ c sugar	

Add:

2 whole beaten eggs	2 pkgs yeast dissolved in
1 t salt	1 c lukewarm water

Mix well, and then add: 4 cups white flour (measured after sifting). Blend well until dough is smooth and gradually add 3½ to 4 cups whole-wheat flour. Blend again until smooth. Cover with wax paper and store in refrigerator overnight in a large greased bowl. It will rise quite a bit in refrigerator. Punch down and divide into two large or four small portions and knead well each one. Put into well-greased loaf pans. Let rise until doubled in bulk — about 3 hours. Bake about 45 minutes in 350-degree oven.

Corn Bread and More

Charlie Hughes

½ lb sausage	1¼ c milk
1 red or green bell pepper, chopped	3 T vegetable oil
1 onion, chopped	1½ c self-rising cornmeal mix
1 egg	

In a 10-inch cast iron skillet, crumble and brown sausage. Add bell pepper and onion to sausage and sauté until tender. Remove mixture from skillet and drain.

Beat egg in a large bowl. Stir in, milk, cornmeal, and sausage mixture. Mix well.

Heat oven to 450 degrees. Wipe skillet clean and add vegetable oil. Heat skillet to almost smoking on stovetop. Pour batter into hot skillet and put it in the oven. Cook for about 20 minutes or until golden brown. Cut into wedges and serve with butter.

Tart Apple Muffins
LaVece Hughes

Muffins:
1 pkg apple cinnamon muffin mix
1 large apple, peeled and diced
⅓ c chopped nuts
3 T brown sugar
5 t flour
1 T margarine, melted

Glaze:
1 c powdered sugar
1 t vanilla
2 T milk

Prepare muffin mix; fold in apples. Fill 6 greased muffins cups ¾ full. Combine nuts, brown sugar, flour and butter; drizzle over batter. Bake at 400 degrees for 15-20 minutes or until lightly browned. Cool for a few minutes, remove from pan.. Combine glaze and drizzle over warm muffins.

Yeast Rolls . . . fantastic
LaVece Ganter Dickinson

3½ c flour
1 pkg dry yeast
1¼ c milk and 1 egg

¼ c sugar
¼ c shortening
1 t salt

In mixing bowl combine 1½ c flour and yeast. Heat milk, sugar, shortening and salt just till warm. Stirring constantly till shortening almost melts. Add to dry mixture. Add egg. Beat at low speed for ½ minute, scraping bowl. Beat 3 minutes at high speed. BY HAND, stir in remaining flour to make a soft ball. Shape into a ball. Place in lightly greased bowl, turn once to grease all surface. Cover and let rise in warm place till double, 1½ to 2 hours. Punch down; turn out on floured surface and cover. Let rest 10 minutes and shape into desired rolls. Dip in melted butter, press in middle with dull blade and cut 2/3 through. Fold over and place in sheet cake pans. Cover with a damp cloth. Let rise in warm place for 30-40 minutes. *"I would go to church and sing in the choir at this point, so the time here could be 1½ hours."* Bake at 400 degrees for 10-12 minutes. 2-3 dozen rolls.

Blue Cheese Biscuits . . . unusual, but good
Kim Overstreet

1 can biscuits
1 stick butter, melted

1 small pkg Blue Cheese

Cut biscuits in fourths and place in a Pyrex dish. Crumble blue cheese on top of biscuits. Pour melted butter over biscuits and bake for 11-13 minutes at 375 degrees.

Corn Bread
LaVece Hughes

3 c self-rising cornmeal
⅓ c sugar
6 eggs

1 ½ c vegetable oil
3 c sour cream
2⅔ c cream-style corn

Combine ingredients in order listed. Mix well. Pour into a greased 9 x 13 pan. Bake at 350 degrees for half hour. Serve with honey butter. To make honey butter, blend 1¼ cups softened butter and ½ cup honey until smooth

Zucchini Bread . . . this is terrific
Jeanne Dickinson White

3 eggs
2 c sugar
2 c shredded zucchini
¾ c oil
1 T vanilla
3 c plain flour

1 T baking powder
2 t cinnamon
1 t baking soda
1 t salt
3 T sesame seed

Beat eggs in large mixing bowl until foamy. Beat in sugar, zucchini, and vanilla. Stir in remaining ingredients except sesame seed. Pour into a 9 x 5 greased and floured pan. Sprinkle with sesame seed. Bake at 350 until done - 1¼ hrs to 1½ hrs. Cool in pan for 10 minutes, remove and cool on wire rack.

Zucchini Squares

LaVece Hughes

3 c shredded zucchini
½ t salt
1 c Bisquick
½ c onion
¼ c oil

½ c Parmesan cheese
2 T parsley
½ t oregano
garlic powder
4 beaten eggs

Mix and spread in greased sheet cake pan. Bake 30 minutes or until brown at 350 degrees.

This is really good and answers the question, "Just what do we do with all this zucchini?

When making griddlecakes, grease the griddle for the first batch. After that rub a piece of raw potato over the hot griddle instead of greasing. The cakes brown nicely and there will be no smoke.
— Betty Hammond

"Whether you are a success or failure in life has little to do with your circumstances; it has much more to do with your choices!"
— Nido Quibien

Salads

Ambrosia . . . dessert or salad
Kate Ganter

oranges
20 oz crushed pineapple

1 pkg frozen crushed coconut
Cool Whip (optional)

Peel the oranges and separate the sections. Peel and seed the sections over a large bowl, so as not to lose any juice. Add pineapple, coconut and a little sugar to taste. Mix well and taste to see if sweet enough. Keep in refrigerator until ready to use. Top with cool whip if desired.

Apple Slaw
LaVece Hughes

Slaw:

Apple Cider vinaigrette:
¼ c apple cider vinegar
2 T salad oil
2 T honey

1 c shredded red cabbage
½ c seedless green or red grapes, halved
⅓ c chopped celery
¼ c slivered almond, toasted
3 c cored, and thinly sliced tart apples

Combine apple cider vinaigrette in a screw top jar. Cover and shake. Combine apples, cabbage, grapes and celery. Shake vinaigrette well and pour over salad, tossing to coat. Cover and chill for 1 hour. Before serving, toss salad with slivered almonds.

Easy Applesauce
LaVece Hughes from Kate Ganter

Select acid cooking apples. Sweet apples will not work. Wash, quarter, and core apples. It is not necessary to peel apples. Place in a large heavy pot and cover with only enough water to barely cover. Stir often to prevent sticking and cook until apples are soft. Run through a "ricer" strainer placed on a large bowl, leaving skins inside and forcing sauce through to bowl. Add sugar, water, and allspice to taste and bring to a boil in a heavy pan. Use in pies, or keep applesauce in refrigerator till used. If canning, place in sterilized jars. (Running through dishwasher will do.) Boil lids and rings and place on top of hot filled jars. Tighten rings, turn upside down for 10 minutes, then right side up to cool until sealed.

Easy because you don't have to peel the apples, just quarter and core them. The ricer strainer can be purchased in a hardware store. It is shaped like a cone and stands in a frame.

Apple Cider Salad
Kate Dickinson Ganter, from the Dickinson's Thanksgiving Dinner

1 small pkg lemon Jell-O
2 c hot apple cider
¼ t salt
1½ T lemon juice

¾ c diced celery, fine
2 large red apples
¼ c chopped pecans

Dissolve Jell-O in hot apple cider; add salt and lemon juice. Chill until slightly thickened. Fold in celery, and apples that have been shredded on coarse side of grater, skin and all. Fold into Jell-O mixture and add nuts. Chill until firm

Asparagus Tomato Salad
LaVece Hughes

1 lb fresh asparagus, trimmed
6 romaine leaves
4 cups torn romaine
⅓ c fat-free Italian salad dressing

12 cherry tomatoes, halved
2 T grated Parmesan cheese
2 hard boiled eggs

In large saucepan, cook asparagus in boiling water for 5-6 minutes until crisp-tender. Place in ice water to stop the cooking. Line 6 plates with romaine leaf and top with torn romaine. Arrange asparagus, tomatoes and eggs on the romaine. Pour dressing over, and sprinkle with cheese.

Beaumont Inn Salad
Lelia Ann Dickinson Smith

1 can white cherries
4 c boiling water
2 cans grapefruit sections
½ c white vinegar
1 large can pineapple chunks

2 c sugar
4 T Knox gelatin
1 t salt
1 c cold water

Soak gelatin in cold water. When dissolved add boiling water and then other ingredients. Pour into mold and arrange fruit when thickened slightly.

Thanks to the Dedmans of Beaumont Inn, Harrodsburg, Kentucky, for permission to include this recipe.

Benedictine Sandwich Spread . . . from the old South

Inez Dickinson from Miss Jennie Benedict, early Louisville caterer

2 6-oz Philadelphia cream cheese
1 t salt or more to taste
mayonnaise to make spreading consistency
grated pulp of 1 medium-sized cucumber

2 or 3 drops of green coloring
1 small onion, grated
dash of Tabasco

Let cheese come to room temperature; mash with a fork. Work into cheese the grated pulp a peeled, medium-sized cucumber, first extracting the juice by straining or placing pulp in paper towel and squeezing it fairly dry-remove large seeds also. Add the onion juices (more if a stronger onion flavor is desired), Tabasco and salt and enough mayonnaise to make a smooth filling easily spread. *(Miss Jennie used mayonnaise made of lemon juice, real olive oil and egg Yolks.)* Add just enough green coloring to give a faint green tinge-- too much will look unappetizing.

Frosted Blueberry Salad

LaVece Hughes

1 15-oz can blueberries
1 pkg (6 oz) sugar free raspberry Jell-O
2 c boiling water
½ c fat free sour cream
½ t vanilla

1 8-oz can unsweetened
    pineapple tidbits
8 oz cream cheese, softened
⅓ c sugar

Drain blueberries and pineapple. Reserve juice, set fruit aside. In bowl dissolve Jell-O in boiling water. Add enough water to juice to make 1 ½ cup. Stir into gelatin. Chill until partially set. Stir in fruit and refrigerate until firm into flat dish. In mixing bowl combine cream cheese and sour cream. Beat in sugar and vanilla. Spread over Jell-O and refrigerate.

Blue Cheese Dressing . . . simple & fantastic

Kate Dickinson Ganter

1 pkg crumbled blue cheese
½ small jar mayonnaise, not
    salad dressing

1 T lemon juice
some chopped onion, optional
sour cream

Mix and adjust to desired consistency with sour cream. Chill if possible.

This is better than any blue cheese dressing you can buy. — lgh

Broccoli Salad
Billie Howard Dickinson and Lelia Ann Dickinson Smith

4 c broccoli
¼ c raisins
8 slices crisp bacon, crumbled
¼ c red onion, chopped

Salad Dressing:
¾ c mayonnaise
2 T vinegar
¼ c sugar

Mix and serve immediately.

Broccoli & Nut Salad
LaVece Hughes

Dressing:
⅓ c red wine vinegar
¼ c sugar
1 c mayonnaise

Salad:
1 pound broccoli
8 oz bacon, crisp and crumbled
1 c toasted pecans or walnuts
1 c seedless red grapes and/or raisins
1 small red onion, thinly sliced

Mix dressing in a capped jar. In large bowl combine broccoli, bacon, nuts, grapes or raisins and onion. Pour dressing and gently mix. Cover and chill for 2-4 hours.

Broccoli & Cauliflower Salad
Barbara Yeast

1 lb broccoli
1 lb cauliflower
½ purple onion
1 jar sunflower seeds

Real bacon bits
¼ c sugar
1 c mayonnaise
2 T apple cider vinegar

Cut broccoli and cauliflower into small pieces. Chop onion. Mix vegetables with sunflower seeds and bacon bits. Mix sugar, mayonnaise, and vinegar and stir into salad.

"Whenever you find that you're on the side of the majority, it's time to reform." — *Mark Twain*

Bing Cherry Salad
Lelia Ann Dickinson Smith

2 pkg cherry flavored Jell-O
2½ c cherry juice (1 can + water)
1 c port wine

1 c chopped pecans
1 c Bing cherries
1 8-oz pkg cream cheese

Dissolve Jell-O in the heated cherry juice and water. Cool and when Jell-O has begun to congeal, add the wine, nuts and cherries. Chill until set.

Topping:
Soften 1 pkg cream cheese with port wine and serve over the top.

Carrot-Raisin Salad
Susan Brown

½ c carrots, shredded
¾ c apple, chopped
⅓ c raisins

1 t   lemon juice
⅓ c Miracle Whip
¼ c slivered almonds, toasted

Combine carrots, apple and raisins. Sprinkle with lemon juice. Sir in Miracle Whip, cover and chill if possible. Sprinkle with almonds before serving, if desired.

Chicken-Almond Salad
Mildred Dickinson

3 c cooked cubed chicken
1½ c chopped celery
3 T lemon juice
1½ c seedless white grapes
¾ c toasted almond slivers

1 t dry mustard
¼ c half and half
1 c mayonnaise
1½ t salt
dash pepper

Combine chicken, celery, and lemon juice. Chill one hour or more. Add grapes and almonds. Combine dressing ingredients and add to mixture. Toss. Garnish with hard-boiled egg slices if desired. Serves eight to ten.

Hawaiian Chicken Salad

LaVece Hughes

1 lb diced, cooked chicken breast
1 green onion, diced
¼ c pineapple chunks
¼ c red papaya chunks
¼ c yellow papaya chunks

¼ c banana slices
1 c pineapple tidbits
1 c mayonnaise
½ c pecans

Stir in mayonnaise and pecans into the other ingredients in a large bowl.

Chicken Salad

LaVece Hughes

2 c torn spinach
2 c torn leaf lettuce
¾ c cubed cooked chicken
⅔ c fresh sliced strawberries

¼ c strawberry-flavored pancake syrup
2 T cider or red wine vinegar
¼ c cashews or pecans
1 orange, peeled and sectioned

Arrange spinach and lettuce on 2 salad plates. Top with chicken, strawberries, and orange sections. Combine syrup and vinegar; drizzle, over salads. Top with nuts.

Coca-Cola Salad

LaVece Hughes

½ c sugar
½ c water
1 c Coca-Cola or Pepsi
1 can dark sweet cherries, pitted

2 small boxes cherry Jell-O
1 small can crushed pineapple
½ c chopped pecans

Mix water, sugar and juices from cherries and pineapple. Boil five minutes. Dissolve Jell-O in the hot mixture and add Coke or Pepsi. Add the nuts and cherries and mix well. Place in the refrigerator until congealed.

Maybe the essence of education is not to stuff you with facts, but to help you discover your uniqueness, to teach you how to develop, and then to show you how to give it away. — Leo Buscaglia

Cornbread Salad

Ethel Fant

Dressing:
1 c mayonnaise
½ c pickle juice
1 T sugar

Salad:
2 c cornbread, crumbled
½ lb bacon, cooked and crumbled
1 Bell pepper, chopped
4 tomatoes, chopped
1 onion, chopped
1 c sweet pickle relish

Crumble cornbread in a 9 x 13 inch pan. Top with mixed vegetables, bacon and pickles, then top with dressing. Refrigerate.

This is best made in advance for several hours or overnight to allow flavors to blend. Will keep for several days

Crabmeat

Selma Dickinson from Mildred Dickinson

2 c crabmeat (3 flat cans
    makes a double recipe)
2 hard boiled eggs, chopped
1 t grated onion
½ t mustard
2 t lemon juice
6-8 scallop shells

1 c Hellmann's mayonnaise
1 t minced fresh parsley
½ t Worcestershire sauce
1 c fine buttered bread
    crumbs
3 T sherry or lemon juice

Pick over crabmeat. Add eggs and all ingredients except half of crumbs. *"I use ½ cup melted butter to 1 cup crumbs."* Fill 6-8 greased scallop shells and top with rest of crumbs. Bake at 400 degrees for 15 minutes. Serve with a lemon wedge and fresh parsley.

You can buy these scallop half-shells at stores such as Pier 1 Imports. My bridge club likes this so much that they won't let me serve anything else.

"Walls turned sideways are bridges."
— Angela Davis

Pea and Tomato Salad
LaVece Hughes

1 chopped onion
1 can small peas, drained

2 chopped tomatoes
½ cup bottled Italian Dressing

Mix and chill.

Corn Salad
Janice Green

2 cans Green Giant Shoepeg corn,
    drained
3 medium tomatoes, chopped coarse
1 c green pepper, diced
juice of 1 lemon

1 c chopped celery
½ c chopped onion
½ c Miracle Whip
salt and pepper

Mix and chill.

Cranberry Congealed Salad . . . holiday favorite
LaVece Hughes

1 pkg plain Knox gelatin
    dissolved in ½ c cold water
1 large black raspberry Jell-O
2 c boiling water
1 carton sour cream

1 can crushed pineapple, juice
    and all
1 can cranberry sauce with
    berries

Dissolve Jell-O in boiling water and add gelatin. Add pineapple with juice. Stir cranberry sauce in can to mix and then add to Jell-O mixture. Pour into 9x13 pan and refrigerate about 1 hour. Stir sour cream and spread on top or swirl into salad.

Cranberry Salad . . . made simple
LaVece Hughes

1 can whole cranberries
1 can crushed pineapple

1 small box cranberry Jell-O
½ c nuts

Mix pineapple and gelatin together in saucepan and let it come to a boil. Remove from heat, add cranberries and nuts. Pour into a mold.

Frozen Cranberry Banana Salad
LaVece Hughes

1 20-oz can pineapple tidbits
5 medium firm bananas,
    halved lengthwise & sliced
16 oz whole berry cranberry sauce

¼ c sugar
12 oz Cool Whip, thawed
½ c chopped nuts

Drain pineapple juice into a medium bowl and set aside. Add sliced bananas to the juice. In large bowl, combine cranberry sauce and sugar. Remove bananas from juice and discard the juice. Add the bananas to the cranberry mixture. Stir in pineapple, cool whip and nuts. Pour into a 13x9 dish and freeze. Serves twelve to sixteen.

Craison Salad (dried cranberries)
LaVece Hughes

1 head red lead lettuce
1 head green lead lettuce
1 head iceberg lettuce
8 oz mozzarella cheese, shredded
1 6-oz pkg Parmesan cheese, shredded
1 c craisins

½ c almonds, sliced
6 chicken breasts, cooked and diced
½ c sweet onion, chopped
½ c red wine vinegar
1 c canola oil
1 lb bacon

Wash lettuces and break into bite sized pieces in a large bowl. Add cheeses, Craisins, bacon, almonds and chicken. In a blender, combine onion, sugar, mustard and red wine vinegar. Blend and slowly add canola oil until well mixed. Pour on salad and toss or serve dressing on the side. Serves eighteen.

Cranberry Salad
Elizabeth Brents Dickinson

1 pkg strawberry gelatin
1 c hot water
1 c sliced raw cranberries

½ c diced celery
½ c chopped nuts

Dissolve gelatin in hot water, add cold water. Chill until slightly thickened. Fold in remaining ingredients. Pour into 1-quart mold. Chill until firm. Serves four to six.

Cranberry Delight
LaVece Hughes

12 oz fresh cranberries
1 c English walnuts, chopped
1 lb grapes, halved and seeded

1 c sugar
1 small container cool whip

Grind cranberries coarsely in food chopper or blender. Add sugar and mix until dissloved. Let stand in refrigerator overnight. The next day, drain for about four hours. Meanwhile, prepare the nuts and grapes. When cranberries have drained, add nuts, grapes and cool whip and blend well. Chill thoroughly. Serves six to eight.

This recipe is adapted from one in the Lexington Herald-Leader. *The lady who sent it in had used it for 20 Years. My family loves it and it is my traditional Christmas dinner salad.*

Curried Fruit
Selma Dickinson from Betsy Martin

1 large can peach halves
1 medium can pear halves
1 medium can pineapple chunks
¾ c brown sugar
⅓ c melted butter

1 T curry powder
½ c blanched slivered almonds
1 small jar maraschino cherries

Drain fruit thoroughly. Spread all except cherries in shallow baking dish. Put a cherry in each pear and peach half. Sprinkle almonds over all. Combine brown sugar, melted butter and the curry powder and top fruit with the mixture. Bake at 325 degrees for 1½ hours. Serves six.

"I've used this recipe at least 1000 times." -- sd

If you are thinking a year ahead, sow seed. If you are thinking 10 years ahead, plant a tree. If you are thinking 100 years ahead, educate the people.
— Kuan-tzu

Four Bean Salad

Kate Ganter From Selma Dickinson

1 c wax beans, drained
1 c cut green beans, drained
1 c whole green beans, drained
1 c red kidney beans, drained
    and washed
1 onion, cut in rings

1 c sugar
1 c vegetable cooking oil
1 c tarragon vinegar (better flavor
    than plain vinegar)
1 green pepper, diced, optional

Cook last three items slightly until sugar is dissolved, then pour over other ingredients and marinate in refrigerator overnight. Less vegetable oil may be used.

Green Salad . . . a family favorite

LaVece Dickinson

1 #2 can crushed pineapple
1 pkg lime Jell-O
1 pkg lemon Jell-O
2 c boiling water
2 c cottage cheese

1 c pineapple juice
¾ c salad dressing
⅓ c chopped pecans
salt

Drain pineapple. Dissolve Jell-O in hot water. Add cold pineapple juice. Add salad dressing and blend with mixer. Pour into flat pans and chill in freezer 15-20 minutes until it freezes around the edges. Turn into mixer and whip until fluffy. Fold in pineapple, cottage cheese and pecans. Chill until firm.

Green Salad

Margaret White from Leslie Webb

1 small pkg lime Jell-O
1 c boiling water
1 c Pet Milk
16 oz crushed pineapple
⅓ c maraschino cherries

¼ c celery
¼ c English walnuts
½ c mayonnaise
1 c cottage cheese

Dissolve Jell-O in boiling water. Cool to room temp. Add remaining ingredients and mix. Chill in serving dish in refrigerator. Top with cherries.

Four Layer Salad . . . a.k.a. sawdust salad

Betty Mulberry, The Ford Cookbook

First layer:
1 pkg orange Jell-O   2 large bananas
1 pkg lemon Jell-O   1 #2 can crushed pineapple, drained
2 c hot water   little marshmallows as needed
1½ c cold water

Dissolve Jell-O in hot water. Add cold water. Add drained pineapple, sliced bananas. Pour into 9 x 13 x 2 pan. Cover with little marshmallows and place in refrigerator to set.

Second layer:
1 c pineapple juice   ½ c sugar
1 whole egg   2 T flour

Combine pineapple juice, egg, and sugar and flour and place into a small saucepan. Cook, stirring constantly over medium heat until thick. Let cool. Spread over first layer.

Third layer:
1 pkg cool whip   8 oz soft cream cheese

Mix cool whip, & cr. cheese until smooth. Spread over second layer.

Fourth layer:
Grated cheddar cheese

Cover the salad with cheese and chill.

Mandarin Orange Salad I

Esther Dickinson

1 small cottage cheese   1 small can crushed pineapple
1 box orange Jell-O   1 small cool whip
1 small can mandarin oranges

Mix cottage cheese and Jell-O powder. Drain oranges and pineapple and add to Jell-O and cottage cheese. Mix in cool whip and refrigerate overnight.

"I have tried to make important ideas trivial." — *Albert Einstein*

Mandarin Orange Salad II
Billie Neal Dickinson and Suetta Wilson Dickinson

1 pkg Jell-O, large, lemon
2 c hot water
1 large can mandarin oranges
2 bananas

1 medium can crushed
   pineapple
1 c miniature marshmallows

Drain oranges and pineapple and reserve juice. Dissolve Jell-O in hot water and add 1½ cups cold orange juice or water. Add orange sections, pineapple, marshmallows and the partially mashed bananas. Let set up in refrigerator and cover with topping.

Topping
½ c pineapple juice
2 T flour
½ c sugar

1 egg
2 T butter

Cook and stir until thick then add 3 oz. cream cheese, cool and add one package of dream whip. Mix and spread over Jell-O.

Mandarin Orange Salad III
Barb Lawler

60 Ritz Crackers, finely crushed
¼ lb margarine, melted
¼ c sugar
1 6-oz can unsweetened frozen
   orange juice
1 can sweetened condensed milk

8 oz cool whip
2 small cans mandarin oranges,
   drained
1 can crushed pineapple, drained
optional: ½ bottle maraschino cherries

Mix crackers crumbs, butter and sugar. Press mixture firmly into a 9 x 13 baking dish, reserving some crumbs for garnish. Blend thawed orange juice with milk. Fold in cool whip, oranges, pineapple, and cherries. Do not beat. Pour mixture over crust. Top with reserved crumbs. Refrigerate or freeze until saving.

*"My dad didn't like me at all. He gave me my allowance
in traveler's checks!" — Rodney Dangerfield*

Orange Delight
LaVece Hughes

2 c water
3 oz orange Jell-O
15 oz mandarin oranges, drained
4 oz Cool Whip

small instant vanilla pudding
small instant tapioca pudding
15 oz crushed pineapple, drained

Bring water to boil. Whisk in gelatin and pudding mixes. Return to boil, stirring constantly. Remove from heat and cool. Fold in oranges and pineapple and cool whip. Spoon into serving bowl. Cool 2 hours.

Orange Fluff Salad
Sherry Dickinson

2 3-oz pkg orange Jell-O
2 c hot water
2 cans mandarin oranges, drained

1 can mandarin oranges drained
1 large can crushed pineapple,
    not drained

Dissolve gelatin in hot water. Stir in orange juice. Cool. Add oranges and pineapple to mixture. Pour in mold and chill.

Topping for Jell-O Salads
LaVece Hughes

1 pkg instant lemon pudding
1 c milk
½ pt whipping cream

Beat pudding mix with milk until slightly firm. Whip cream and fold into pudding. Spread on gelatin.

> *Great truths about life that adults have learned:*
> *—Raising teenagers is like nailing Jell-O to a tree.*
> *—Families are like fudge . . . mostly sweet, with a few nuts.*
> *—Today's mighty oak is just yesterday's nut that held its ground.*
> *—Laughing is good exercise. It's like jogging on the inside.*
> *— Beth Brock*

Bread and Butter Pickles
Aunt Gwendolyn Dickinson

10 medium cucumbers, thinly sliced
6 medium onions, sliced
2 medium green peppers, sliced

Add ½ cup salt and 2 trays of ice to above. Soak 2 hours with weighted lid. Combine the following and bring to boil:

1½ c sugar
1¾ c water
½ t turmeric

1½ t each of mustard seed,
celery seed, and ginger
2 c vinegar

Drain the cucumbers, etc. and add to the mixture. Simmer, stirring occasionally until the cucumbers have lost their bright green color. Do not boil, simmer only. Pack in hot sterilized jars and seal. Makes 5 pints.

Candied Sweet Pickles
LaVece Dickinson from Inez Dickinson

1 qt cheap whole sweet pickles
2 c sugar

Cut pickles in 4 spears each. Put pickle juice into a pan and bring to a boil. Meanwhile put spears back into their jar by lying jar on side and packing them in. Sprinkle 2 cups of sugar over the top of the spears. Shake it down. May have to push sugar down into the jar with a knife. Add ¼ teaspoon celery seed, several whole cloves, and 1 broken cinnamon stick. Pour hot juice over pickles until reaches the top of jar. Close lid and gently turn until sugar dissolves. Chill. Chop and use in potato salad.

A quick and inexpensive way to make candied sweet pickles.

Lime Pickles . . . exceptional

Betty Cecil Hughes

7 lbs cucumbers	2 c pickling lime
(about 4" long)	2 gal water

Cut cucumbers in slices and soak in crock, not a plastic container, with pickling lime and water for 24 hours. Mixture will separate and should be mixed with hand 3-4 times. After 24 hours rinse several times in cool clear water and soak in cool clear water for 3 hours. Mix the following in a large pot:

2 qt vinegar	1 t mixed pickling spice
4½ lbs sugar	½ T salt

Put pickles in pot and simmer for 35 minutes and put in sterile jars. Jars may be cleaned by running through the dishwasher. Boil lids and rings and place on hot pickle jars. Place rings around lids and tighten down. Let cool upside down for 10 minutes, turn right side up and jars will seal.

These are the best sweet pickles you will ever eat. My friend Stephen Holthaus was moved to praise these pickles in song. —lgh

*I don't want a pickle
jus' wanna ride my motor-sickle*

*And I don't wanna die
jus wanna ride my motor-sie*

*But that's all changed since I ate your pickles
Don't really care about them motor-sickles*

*Don't really care even if I die
long as I have one of them pickles 'fore I say goodbye*

— With apologies from Stephen Holthaus to Arlo Guthrie.

Sweet Pickle Relish
Betty Cecil Hughes

12 medium cucumbers
3 medium onions
2 red sweet peppers
2 green sweet peppers
2 T salt

1½ c vinegar
2½ c sugar
1½ t celery seed
1½ t mustard seed

Grind together cucumbers, onions and peppers, using coarse blade. Sprinkle with salt. Let stand 3 hours. Drain. In large kettle combine vinegar, sugar, celery seed and mustard seed. Bring just to boiling. Add cucumber mixture and simmer 20 minutes. Pack lightly in sterilized jars. Seal immediately. Makes about 3 pints.

Pistachio Salad . . . quick, and good
Inez Dickinson

3½ oz instant pistachio
    pudding mix
8 oz crushed pineapple

1 large cool whip
½ c chopped nuts
1 c miniature marshmallows

Mix together and refrigerate. Best if refrigerated overnight.

This salad is also called "Five Cup Salad" or "Watergate Salad".— lgh

Creamy Herb Dressing
LaVece Hughes

1 pkg Hidden Valley Ranch mix
1 qt mayonnaise
1½ pound sour cream
1½ cups buttermilk
1½ cups whole milk
⅓ t ground mustard

salad greens

1 c diced tomatoes
½ c bacon bits

Combine first six ingredients and mix. Before serving salad, add to greens and toss with diced tomatoes and heated bacon bits.

Salad Dressing . . . for fruit salad
Selma Dickinson from Lucie Porter Dickinson

1 stick butter (melted)
1 pt mayonnaise
¼ c chopped parsley

½ t garlic powder
½ t curry powder
½ t marjoram

Mix well. Shred lettuce on plate. Layer with diced chicken breast, then dressing. Top with sliced almonds. Serve with fresh fruit and hot rolls. Good especially with peaches, strawberries, and white grapes.

Red French Dressing
LaVece Hughes

1 c ketchup
1 c vegetable oil
¾ c sugar or sugar substitute
1 T vinegar

1 t garlic salt
¼ t pepper
2 T Parmesan cheese

Combine all ingredients in a quart jar. Tighten lid. Shake well, and refrigerate.

¼ cup oil works well also. Makes a great diet dressing. -- lgh

Shrimp Mold Supreme
Billie Howard Dickinson

2 7½-oz cans shrimp
1 can tomato soup, undiluted
1 c mayonnaise
1 c celery, chopped fine

1 8-oz pkg cream cheese
1 c onion, chopped fine
2 T unflavored gelatin

Drain shrimp and save liquid. Flake shrimp. Soak gelatin in ½ cup of shrimp liquid. Heat soup and cream cheese. Beat with mixer until cheese is fully melted and mixture is smooth. Pour soup mixture into gelatin, and then add mayonnaise, shrimp, celery and onion. Mix well. Pour into mold and refrigerate until firm.

Don't agonize, organize!

Pineapple Slaw . . . I really like this
LaVece Hughes

2-3 c shredded cabbage
1-2 T milk
2 T vinegar

1 8-oz can pineapple tidbits, drained
2 T sugar

Combine mayonnaise, vinegar, sugar and milk. Place cabbage and pineapple in a large bowl; add dressing and toss.

Sumi Salad . . . oriental slaw
Billie Neal Dickinson and Liz Moore

1 head chopped cabbage
6 T sesame seed (toasted)
6 T slivered almonds (toasted)
2 pkgs Ramen noodles,
    (uncooked and broken
      into pieces)
4 green onions (chopped)

Dressing:
6 t wine vinegar
2 T sugar
⅔ c oil
1 t pepper
pinch of salt

Make dressing and combine ingredients just prior to serving. Best before noodles soften.

Yogurt-Blue Cheese Dressing
Joan Dickinson Walker

1 carton plain yogurt
¼ c mayonnaise
1 or 2 oz crumbled blue cheese

1 T salt
¼ t ground pepper

Combine and mix well.

> *Great truths about life, that little children have learned:*
>   *—You can't hide a piece of broccoli in a glass of milk.*
>   *—Don't wear polka-dot underwear under white shorts.*
>   *—The best place to be when you're sad is Grandma's lap.*
>   *— Beth Brock*

Pea and Peanut Salad ... unusual but very good
Jeanne Dickinson White

⅓ c mayonnaise
¼ t dill
¼ t dry mustard
½ t sugar
2 T sour cream
½ t vinegar

10-oz pkg frozen peas
1 c Spanish peanuts

Combine dressing ingredients several hours or overnight in advance and refrigerate. Thaw peas and combine with peanuts. Add dressing just before serving.

Peas with Oranges and Cashews
LaVece Hughes

½ c Miracle Whip
2 T milk
1 t lemon juice
1 10-oz pkg baby sweet peas,
    cooked, drained and cooled

3 green onions, thinly sliced
1 11-oz can mandarin oranges
¼ c cashew pieces
1 t sugar

Blend Miracle Whip, milk, lemon juice, and sugar in a medium bowl. Add peas, onions and oranges. Toss gently. Refrigerate 4-6 hrs. Sprinkle with cashews before serving.

Pineapple-Nut Salad
LaVece Hughes

1 can crushed pineapple
½ c pecans
½ c cherries

8 oz Kool Whip
8 oz cream cheese
2 T sugar or substitute

Beat cream cheese with juice from pineapple until smooth and fluffy. Stir in remaining ingredients.

For several years I've been getting this tasty salad off the Kroger salad bar. I think I've finally figured out how to make it. – lgh

Pineapple & Rice
LaVece Hughes

1 c white rice, cooked
   (may use Minute Rice
    but other is best)
¾ c white sugar

½ stick margarine
1 20-oz can crushed pineapple
   in its own juice
1 whole egg, beaten

While rice is cooking in saucepan, mix sugar, margarine and pineapple. Cook until mixture boils and remove heat. Let cool to lukewarm. Add beaten egg and rice and stir. *This is good as a leftover when heated. If too thick, add a little milk.*

Baked Potato Salad
LaVece Hughes

1 lb potatoes
¼ c chopped onion
¼ c chopped celery
2 t pimento
salt and pepper to taste

½ c mayonnaise
1 t mustard
1 t milk
2 slices bacon, crisp and crumbled

Peel potatoes, dice into ¾ in cubes and boil until tender enough to pierce with a fork. Drain and cool. In small bowl, mix mayonnaise, mustard and milk and set aside. Cook bacon, drain, and crumble. In large bowl, mix cooled potatoes, celery, onion, bacon, pimento and mayonnaise mixture. Salt and pepper to taste.

Potato Salad
LaVece Dickinson

Cook red potatoes, peeled and cut into ½-inch cubes. Cook until done, but not mushy. Drain potatoes and marinate with a mixture of 2-3 tablespoons of oil and 1 tablespoon of lemon juice until cool, then add:

chopped celery
chopped candied sweet pickles,
   onion, and diced parsley

mayonnaise (not salad dressing)
salt
optional: sprinkle with paprika.

Potato Salad With Yogurt

Ann Dickinson Beal

Boil potatoes either in or out of jackets, depending on your persuasion. Drain and cut into small pieces before they are completely cooled. Sprinkle with a tablespoon or so of wine vinegar. When cooled, add:

chopped celery
chopped green onions
chopped parsley
chopped green pepper

chopped green pepper
any other fresh veggies which are
    available (snow peas are great)
yogurt and mayonnaise

Mix vegetables together with a cup or so of plain yogurt and a dollop or two of mayonnaise and salt and pepper to taste.

"This is especially good with new garden potatoes."

Red, White, & Blue Salad

Fran Dickinson

2 3-oz pkg Raspberry Jell-O
3 c hot water
1 envelope plain gelatin
½ c cold water
1 c sugar

1 t vanilla
1 8-oz pkg cream cheese
1 c coffee cream
½ c chopped nuts
1 can (#303) blueberries and juice

First layer:
1 pkg raspberry Jell-O dissolved in 2 c hot water. Pour into an 8 x 12 pan and let set.

Second layer:
Soften plain gelatin in cold water. Heat on low, heat the coffee cream with sugar; combine with gelatin. Add vanilla, softened cream cheese and chopped nuts. Put on top of first layer.

Third layer:
After second layer is firm, combine 1 pkg raspberry gelatin with 1-cup hot water and add blueberries, juice and all. Put on top of second layer. Put in refrigerator until firm.

A kind word is never lost. It keeps on going from one person to another, until it comes back to you!

Sauerkraut Slaw . . . unusual, and good

Jane Tyler

½ c sugar
1 can sauerkraut

1 c sliced onion
1 c sliced green pepper

Mix together and let stand overnight.

Jane gave me this recipe at the Crestwood Christian Church and Bethesda Baptist Church Interfaith Dialogue Picnic. — lgh

Strawberry Pretzel Salad

LaVece Hughes

2 c thin pretzels, broken
    into small pieces
1 stick butter melted
4 T sugar & 1 c sugar
8 oz cool whip, thawed
8 oz cream cheese

6 oz strawberry Jell-O
2 cups boiling water
½ c cold water
16 oz frozen strawberries

Crust:
Combine pretzels, margarine and 4 tablespoons sugar. Pat into a greased 9 x 13 pan. Bake at 325 degrees for 10 minutes. Let cool.

First Layer:
Make middle layer by combining cool whip with cream cheese and 1 cup sugar. Pour into cooled crust.

Top Layer:
Combine Jell-O with water and strawberries. When thick, pour on top of cream cheese layer. Chill until set.

"Sometimes our light goes out, but it is blown into flame by another human being. Each of us owes deepest thanks to those who have rekindled this light."
— Albert Schweitzer

Spinach Salad with Red Dressing
Mary Mc Murray

Dressing:
1 c oil
¾ c sugar
⅓ c ketchup
¼ vinegar
1 t Worcestershire sauce
Sprinkle tarragon and garlic

Salad:
1 bag of baby spinach
1 can bean sprouts, drained
1 medium red onion, diced
⅓ c slivered almonds
8 slices bacon, cooked and crumbled
3 hard-boiled eggs, diced

Make dressing ahead of time. Mix with rest just before serving.

I substitute artificial sweetner for the sugar. — lgh

Strawberry Cream Squares . . . a family favorite
Lelia Ganter Handy

2 3-oz pkgs strawberry Jell-O
2 c boiling water
2 10-oz pkgs frozen strawberries

1 13½-oz can crushed pineapple
2 large bananas
1-2 c sour cream

Dissolve Jell-O in boiling water. Add frozen strawberries, and stir occasionally till thawed. Add pineapple and bananas, finely chopped. Pour half into 9 x 13 x 2 pan. Chill until firm. Spread evenly with sour cream. Cover with remainder of Jell-O mixture. Chill

Veggie Potato Salad
LaVece Hughes

1 lb potatoes, cooked and cubed
¼ c chopped red onion
⅓ c fat-free Italian salad dressing
¼ t dill weed

1½ c chopped fresh broccoli
½ c diced celery
2 T chopped green pepper
½ t salt free Seasoning Blend

In a large bowl, toss potatoes and veggies. In a small bowl, blend salad dressing and seasonings. Add to potato mixture and toss. Cover and refrigerate for 1 hour or more. *"I often leave the skins on the potatoes."*

Vegetable Salad
Lelia Ganter Handy

Salad:
1 c LeSeur peas
1 c shoepeg white corn
⅓ c chopped green onions
1 c French cut green beans

Dressing:
¾ c sugar
¾ c vinegar
1 c oil, "scant"
1 t salt & pepper

Drain all vegetables. Mix dressing, pour over vegetables and mix. Better after 24 hours. Keeps for two weeks refrigerated.

"I usually use small cans of the vegetables. Also, instead of the dressing, I often use 1/2 to 1 c of "bought" Italian salad dressing to which I add about 2 tablespoons of sugar."

Waldorf Salad Supreme
LaVece Hughes

3 Granny Smith apples
3 red delicious apples
Miracle Whip

1 can drained crushed pineapple
1 c chopped nuts
1 c raisins

Pare apples, but don't peel. Cut into small pieces. Add nuts, raisins, and pineapple. Mix with enough Miracle Whip to moisten and refrigerate if time permits.

"My friend Lo Arnold's addition of the pineapple to this old salad from the Waldorf Hotel makes this a special salad."— lgh

Weight Watcher's Fruit Salad
Sice Shanklin

1 can of fruit cocktail, light
1 can of pineapple tidbits, light
1 can of pears, light

1 small pkg of fat free, sugar-
  free vanilla pudding

Using same size cans of fruit, drain and mix together. Pour dry pudding on top and mix well. Refrigerate overnight. Just before serving may add fresh bananas, strawberries or blueberries.

I often add to this easy combination whatever fruit I have at hand. — lgh

White Salad
Barb Lawler

2 pkgs unflavored gelatin
¼ cu cold water
1 8-oz pkg cream cheese
⅔ c chopped walnuts

1 large can crushed pineapple
1 c sugar
1 c of cool whip

Boil sugar and pineapple mixture for 5 minutes. Dissolve gelatin in cold water and stir into pineapple mixture. Chill until the consistency of unbeaten egg whites. Soften cream cheese and whip until smooth. Add chopped walnuts. Fold in cool whip. Refrigerate.

Fruit Salad
Jerry Wietzel

1 small box vanilla pudding
1 can pineapple tidbits, drained
1 can mandarin oranges, drained
1-2 c white grapes

1 c cool whip
1 c small marshmallows
1 c chopped nuts

Cook pudding with 1½ c of the juice from the fruits instead of milk. Cool. Add cool whip, fruit, nuts and marshmallows.

Napa Cabbage Slaw . . . a real hit
Patsy Alexander Nielsen

2 lb head cabbage, chopped
2 c Chinese noodles or 2 pkg dry Ramen noodles, crushed
5-6 green onions, finely chopped
¾ cup slivered almonds, toasted
¼ c toasted sesame or sunflower seeds

Mix and place in large salad bowl. Add dressing just before serving.

Dressing:
⅓ c oil
3-6 T soy sauce
1 c white vinegar

1 c sugar (or equiv amount of
   artificial sweetner)
½ t salt

Fruits & Vegetables

Cheese Apples
LaVece Hughes

2 cans Luck Apples
¼ c water
1 T lemon juice
⅔ c sugar
½ c flour

¼ c butter
¾ c grated cheese
½ t cinnamon
½ t nutmeg

Place apples, water, lemon juice, cinnamon and nutmeg in a baking dish. Mix sugar, flour, butter and grated cheese until crumbly. Put on top of apples and bake at 350 for 1 hour. Serves six.

Baked Apples
LaVece Hughes

4 large Granny Smith apples,
  unpeeled and quartered
1 c sugar

1 t cinnamon
1 T cornstarch
¼ c butter, cut into pieces

Quarter unpeeled apples into a baking dish. Mix together dry ingredients. Sprinkle dry mixture over apples. Dot with butter. Bake covered at 350 degrees for about 45 minutes. Makes four to six servings.

Asparagus Casserole . . . a family favorite
Lelia Ann Dickinson Smith

1½ c cracker crumbs
½ c melted margarine
2 cans asparagus, drained
½ c slivered almonds
3 T flour

1½ c milk
1 t salt
4 T margarine
1 glass Kraft Old English Cheese
  or your favorite cheese

Line bottom of baking dish with a cup of buttered crumbs. Add drained asparagus, then almonds. Make sauce of 4 tablespoons of margarine, flour, milk, and salt (Cook in microwave for 2 minutes, remove and stir and cook for 2 minutes more until bubbling and thick.) Add cheese and mix. Pour over asparagus and top with remaining crumbs. Bake at 450 degrees for twelve minutes.

Tact is the unsaid part of what your think.

Quick Baked Beans . . . cooked the U.S. Army way

LaVece Hughes, from Chef Leon at Winburn

1 small can of baked beans
1 T Worcestershire sauce
2 T margarine

4 bacon strips cut into small pieces
2 T minced onions
¼ c tomato ketchup

Combine margarine and ketchup and boil until it thickens. Drain baked beans and add to mixture with remaining ingredients. Boiling before adding the beans is a way to get a thick consistency without risk of scorching the beans.

This quick way to make good baked beans was given to me by a former Army cook. Of course, I had to scale it down a bit. — lgh

Sauce for Broccoli . . . mock Hollandaise

Lelia Ganter Handy

Mix: ½ c mayonnaise
2½ T mustard

Mix and serve on top of cooked broccoli.

So easy and sooo good. — lgh

Broccoli Soup . . . a family favorite

Heidi Bowkamp

38-oz bag frozen broccoli
    or broccoli and cauliflower

3 diced potatoes, no need to peel
1 qt water, or more

Boil 20 minutes and add:

2 cubes chicken bouillon
1½ lb Velveeta cheese

2 cans cream of celery soup or
    cream of chicken soup

Cook over low heat until cheese is thoroughly melted.

Adjust consistency with water; I like it very thick. Much better than anything that you can buy, and easy, too. — lgh

U.S. Capitol Bean Soup
Served each day of the year in all eleven Capitol dining rooms

1 lb dry white beans, soaked
    overnight (or quick soaked)
1 meaty ham bone or 2 smoked
    ham hocks
3 qts water
3 onions, finely chopped
3 cloves garlic, finely chopped

4 stalks celery, with leaves,
    finely chopped
¼ c parsley, finely chopped
salt and pepper to taste

Senate version:
Thicken with 1 c mashed potatoes

Strain the water from the soaked beans and put in a big pot with 3 qts of water and the ham bone or ham hocks. Bring to boil, then reduce heat and simmer for 2 hours. Stir the chopped vegetables and herbs into the pot, and also the mashed potatoes if you're cooking the Senate version, then cook over low heat for another hour until the beans are tender. Remove the bones from the pot; cut the meat into small pieces and return the meat to the pot. Ladle into bowls.

For "U.S. House of Representative Bean Soup" authenticity, crush a few of the beans in each bowl to thicken the broth and make it slightly opaque.

Corn Pudding . . . from *Ford's Favorite Recipes*
Virginia Shay, via Betty Mulberry

Combine:
½ c self-rising flour
¼ c sugar

Mix and Add:
4 eggs
2 c fresh corn, *or*
    1 can cream style white
    shoepeg corn and
    1 can whole corn drained

Add:
1 c half and half
1 stick butter melted in dish you
    intend to use for baking

Pour butter into rest of corn mixture and return to baking dish. Sprinkle with nutmeg and cook in a 350 degree oven for 45 minutes until brown and pulls away from the edge.

If you don't have creamed corn, put a drained can of corn into the blender and you have a can of creamed corn. — lgh

Never-Fail Corn Pudding
LaVece Hughes

2 c whole-kernel corn
2 T white sugar
2 large eggs
1 T flour

1 c milk
salt and pepper
1 T margarine

Mix in dish you bake it in. No need to grease. Bake for 45 minutes at 350 degrees.

Microwave Corn Pudding
LaVece Hughes

1 c milk
¼ c margarine
¼ c sugar
1 t salt
¼ c flour

17-oz can corn, drained
1 egg, slightly beaten
dash of pepper
nutmeg

Place 2 T margarine in deep 1 qt heat resistant casserole. Heat, uncovered on high for 30-45 seconds. Blend flour, salt, pepper and sugar. Microwave on high for 1 minute or until bubbly. Gradually add milk, stirring constantly. Add corn and egg. Blend thoroughly. Sprinkle nutmeg on top. Microwave uncovered on medium high for 13-14 minutes or until set. Stir after 6 minutes. Serves six.

Fried Corn
Bobbi Jo Yeast

1 bag frozen Shoepeg corn or
    fresh corn
2 T sugar or more to your taste
1 t salt

1 t pepper
2-3 strips bacon
1-2 T flour
water

Cook bacon and cut into small pieces. Leave in skillet with grease. Pour corn in skillet. Add sugar, salt, pepper and water to cover. Let simmer for about an hour. When corn is tender, mix flour with water and pour into corn mixture. Simmer about 10-15 more minutes. Serve with tomato slices.

Corn *Au Jus* . . . naturally
Martha Dickinson

Leave fresh corn ears in their husks. Don't even peep to look for worms. Do not remove tassels. Cook on high in microwave oven, two to five minutes per ear. Let ears sit a few minutes and cool. Remove husks, tassels and worms. Add nothing. Enjoy corn steamed in its own juices *Simple, but delicious!*

Curried Pumpkin Soup
LaVece Hughes

½ lb fresh mushrooms, sliced	15 oz solid pack pumpkin
½ c chopped onion	1 can evaporated milk
2 T butter	1 T honey
2 T flour	½ t salt
¾ t curry powder	¼ t pepper
3 c vegetable broth	¼ t ground nutmeg

In a large saucepan, sauté the mushrooms and onion in butter until tender. Stir in the flour and curry powder until blended. Gradually add the broth. Bring to a boil; cook and stir for 2 minutes or until thickened. Add the pumpkin, milk, honey, salt, pepper and nutmeg. Heat. Garnish with chives if desired. Serves 7.

Green Bean Almandine
Susan Spears Hughes

1 bag frozen green beans	½ t lemon pepper
½ cup slivered almonds	3 T butter
juice from 1 lemon	

Microwave green beans until desired doneness. In a small pan melt butter, stir in lemon juice. Add lemon pepper and almonds. Cook over medium heat until almonds are toasted. Pour over green beans.

Neither brains nor ingenuity will take the place of hard work.

Green Beans and Potatoes . . . good and easy.
LaVece Hughes

28 oz green beans   1 pkg onion soup mix   8-10 new potatoes

Drain beans, and place in big saucepan of water with potatoes and onion soup mix. Bring to a boil, lower heat and cook until potatoes are done and beans are cooked down.

Grits Casserole
Emmy Lou Dickinson

1 c instant grits
5 c boiling salted water
1 stick butter
1½ 6-oz rolls cheese,
    garlic or sharp

2 eggs, beaten
½ c milk
Optional:
    2 c corn flakes, crushed
    2 T. butter, melted

Cook grits in water slowly for 20 minutes or until thick, stirring often. Melt butter and cheese in grits. Beat 2 eggs in a cup and finish filling cup with milk. Let grits cool and add egg mixture. Pour into greased casserole. Top with corn flakes that have been mixed with butter. Makes 2½ quarts. Cook at 350 degrees for 45 minutes. Will freeze.

From My Cousin's Kitchen *a cookbook that Emmy Lou wrote with her sister, Jo Brent Miller Robertson of Lexington, and her cousin, Jean Smith Jewell Claiborne of Owensboro. — lgh*

Lima Beans Casserole
LaVece Hughes

1 box frozen lima beans
1 box frozen chopped broccoli
1 can water chestnuts
1 c sour cream

1 can cream of mushroom soup
2 T melted butter
12 crushed crackers

Cook limas and broccoli according to package directions just until tender. You can cook both in same pan, but start limas first, then the broccoli, so they will be done at the same time. Mix all remaining ingredients (except crackers and butter) with the limas and broccoli and add ¼ c water. Spread mixture into a shallow baking dish and top with crackers mixed with butter. Bake at 350 degrees for 40-45 minutes or until bubbly. Can make the day before; add crackers before baking.

Mushroom Soup . . . from my Mom

Mary Lou Stapleton Dickinson

1 lb white, large mushrooms
salt and pepper
3 T butter
onion to flavor

flour to thicken
1 clove garlic or garlic powder
Orzo (noodles shaped like eggs)

Clean mushrooms and cut a little off the stem. Place in pot filled with cold water (1½ - 2 quarts). Cook about half hour until tender. Leave juice in pot and take out mushrooms. Dice mushrooms. In frying pan, melt butter and lightly sauté onion. Add flour until butter is absorbed. Keep stirring to prevent burning. Bring to a medium brown. Don't let it dry or be soupy. Add a few drops of water (¼ c of mushroom water) to flour. Heat to gravy consistency and then add to mushroom water. Pour in slowly and stir until all is mixed. Strain out onions. Placed diced mushrooms back in liquid. Serve with rice shaped noodles (Orzo) mixed into heated soup.

Sweet Vidalia Onion Casserole

Lelia Ganter Handy from Shelby Bale

2 c water
1 c rice
6 large onions
dash paprika
1 c whipping cream

½ c butter
2 T minced fresh parsley
¼ t white pepper
1 c shredded Swiss cheese
¼ t salt

Bring water to boil, cook rice, and simmer for 10 minutes. Peel, quarter, and chop onions. Melt butter in Dutch oven over medium heat. Add onions and cool 15 minutes, stirring often. Remove from heat and add rest of ingredients. Spoon into lightly greased 13 x 9 baking dish. Cover and bake at 350 degrees for 30 minutes. Lightly sprinkle with paprika.

Vidalia Onion Bake

John Johnson

Peel onions. Place a pat of butter and a bullion cube on each onion. Seal each onion individually in Reynolds Wrap. Bake for 1 hour at 450 degrees.

Pineapple Casserole . . . simply marvelous
Susan Sallee from Lisa Ward

2 cans pineapple, one chunk and
    one crushed (drained)
1 c sugar

¼ c flour
2 rolls Ritz crackers, crushed
2 sticks butter

Mix pineapple, sugar and flour, and place in baking dish. Mix crackers and butter, and place on top of pineapple mixture. Bake 30-40 minutes at 350 degrees.

Easy, and a really fantastic dish with any chicken or special dinner. — lgh

Sweet Potato Casserole
Loetta Arnold

2 lrg cans sweet potatoes, drained
1 c sugar
1 stick butter, melted
1 T vanilla

½ t cinnamon or pumpkin pie spice
3 large eggs
½ c half and half

Whip everything together with mixer. Pour into greased 9 x 13 casserole and bake for 30 minutes at 350 degrees.

Topping:
1 pound brown sugar
⅓ c butter

1 stick butter
1 c chopped pecans or walnuts

Mix sugar, flour and butter, together. (Should be crumbly). Add nuts. Sprinkle on top of casserole as soon as it comes from the oven. Return to oven for 10 minutes.

Rice Casserole
Sherry Dickinson

1 medium onion chopped fine
1 can mushrooms (stems,
    pieces and liquid)

2 cans beef consommé
2 c minute rice
1 stick butter

Pour rice in casserole; add onion, mushrooms and slice butter over top. Cook 45 minutes, stirring 3 or 4 times. Bake at 350 degrees. *Good with chicken or replaces potatoes.*

Green Rice
Janice Underwood

½ c chopped celery
½ c chopped onion
16 oz chopped broccoli

8 oz Velveeta or cheese whiz
1 can cream of chicken soup
1 c uncooked instant or wild rice

Sauté celery and onion in butter in saucepan. Remove from heat and add cheese and soup. Stir, cover and let sit. While cheese melts prepare rest of ingredients. In another pan cook broccoli according to pkg directions. When broccoli is cooked, turn off heat and add instant rice. Stir, cover and let sit until rice absorbs water. Mix both pans together. Pour into casserole dish and bake at 350 degrees for about 25 - 30 minutes.

This is one of my favorite vegetable casserole recipes. -- lgh

Oriental Rice Casserole
Lelia Ann Dickinson Smith

4 c cooked rice
1 c drained bean sprouts
½ c diagonally sliced celery
¼ c chopped green pepper
½ c Italian dressing

1 c sliced water chestnuts
2 pimentos
1 ½ lb. cooked shrimp
2 green onions
¼ c soy sauce

In a large bowl combine rice, bean sprouts, celery, green pepper, pimentos, water chestnuts and shrimp. Chill. Combine dressing and soy sauce. Pour over salad mixture

Stewed Tomatoes
Wynette from Wynette's Family Restaurant in Harrodsburg, KY

2 lb can tomatoes
2 cups sugar

Several left-over biscuits

Place tomatoes in large pan and *"smash them."* Add sugar and leftover biscuits. Cook on top of stove until mixed and cooked down.

Stop by Wynette's some time and try her marvelous Coconut Pie.

*According to the Cigna Life Insurance Company
smiling lowers your blood pressure.*

Tomato Pie . . . unusual, but very good
Lelia Ganter Handy

Bake a pie shell for 10 minutes at 450 degrees. Boil 3-4 medium tomatoes for 30 seconds and remove skins

Prepare cheese mixture:
½ c or more mayonnaise   1 t oregano
2 c grated cheddar cheese   1 t chives
1 t basil

Cut tomatoes and place in cooked pie shell. Place cheese mixture over tomatoes. Sprinkle ½ c mozzarella cheese over pie. Bake 350 degrees for 25-30 minutes.

Vegetable Casserole
LaVece Hughes

15 oz white corn   1 can cream of mushroom soup
15 oz French style green   ½ lb Velveeta
    beans   ½ t salt and pepper
1 c sour cream   2 c crackers, crumbled
½ c chopped onion   ½ stick butter
½ t seasoned salt   8 oz sliced mushrooms

Drain corn, green beans, and mushrooms. Melt cheese and butter separately. Combine first 9 ingredients and place into 9 x13 baking dish. Top with crackers and butter. Bake for 75 minutes in a 350-degree oven.

Taco Limas
LaVece Hughes

2 cans white limas   1 4-oz can taco sauce
2-3 pieces of bacon, fried and   ½ green pepper, diced
    crumbled 1 small onion, diced

Sauté onion and pepper in bacon grease. Mix ingredients. Put in buttered casserole. Heat 45 minutes at 350 degrees

Vegetable Strata
Jeanne White

40 oz frozen broccoli
½ lb mushrooms sliced
¼ c + 2 T margarine, divided
½ c mayonnaise
½ c sour cream
½ c grated Parmesan

8½-oz can artichoke hearts,
    drained and quartered
salt and pepper
3 tomatoes, or 14 oz can
½ c seasoned bread crumbs

Cook broccoli and drain. Sauté mushrooms in 2 T margarine. Combine mayonnaise, sour cream and Parmesan. Stir in artichokes, broccoli and mushrooms. Season with salt and pepper. Pour into 9 x 13 casserole, greased. Slice tomatoes ½" thick and place over mixture. Melt ¼ cup margarine, stir in breadcrumbs, and sprinkle over casserole. Bake at 325 degrees for 30 minutes.

Zucchini Casserole
Mildred Dickinson

1 c sliced onion rings
1 c sliced green pepper
¼ c butter
salt and pepper to taste

¼ c grated parmesan cheese
2 c zucchini slices
4 fresh tomatoes peeled and
    cut into wedges

Sauté onions and green pepper in butter until light brown. Add zucchini slices and cook 5 minutes more. Add tomatoes. Cook 5 minutes stirring occasionally. Season with salt and pepper. Pour into casserole. Top with the Parmesan cheese and a few buttered cracker crumbs. Bake in 325-degree oven for 30 minutes. Serves 8.

Italian Green Beans
Kate Ganter

2 small cans green beans, drained
1 medium onion
1 can stewed tomatoes or
    tomato sauce

bacon, fried crisp and crumbled
1 T butter or bacon drippings

Put all in stew kettle and boil down until juice is low.

Squash Casserole
Sondra Bowman Dickinson

2 c cooked squash
½ stick melted butter
½ c evaporated milk
2 t flour
1 t salt

¼ t pepper
1 egg, well beaten
1¼ c grated cheese
1 t sugar

Mix ingredients and place in baking dish top with buttered cracker crumbs. Cook at 350 degrees till it bubbles up or crumbs are slightly brown.

Summer Squash Casserole
Ann Burns

6 c sliced summer squash
¼ c chopped onion
1 c shredded carrot (opt)
1 can cream of chicken soup
Parmesan cheese

1 c low-fat sour cream
8-oz pkg Pepperidge Farm herb
    stuffing mix
½ c melted margarine

Cook squash and onion in boiling salted water for 5 minutes. Drain. Combine soup and sour cream and fold into veggies. Combine stuffing and butter. Spread ½ on bottom of 12 x 7 ½ x 2 baking dish. Spread vegetable mixture and top with remaining stuffing. Sprinkle Parmesan cheese on top. Bake for 25-30 minutes at 350 degrees.

"This is a really good way to use up summer squash. I have served it to large groups by doubling it. Ann took it from the University of Kentucky's Green Thumb Cookbook.

Beets . . . can't be beat
Faye Smith

3 T sugar
1 T corn starch

½ c orange juice

Cook till thickened, then add 1 can beets, drained and heat until warmed.

I thought that there was no way that beets could be prepared that would be tasty. Faye's recipe proved me wrong. — lgh

76

Broccoli Casserole . . . a family favorite
Emmy Lou Dickinson, from My Cousin's Kitchen

10 oz pkg chopped broccoli
1 c mayonnaise
1 c grated cheddar cheese
1 can cream of celery or
    cream of mushroom soup

2 T butter, melted
2 T onion, minced
2 eggs, beaten
½ c crushed Ritz crackers or herb
    stuffing mix

Cook broccoli according to package directions. Drain well. Combine all the ingredients and place in casserole. Cover with cracker crumbs and butter. Bake at 350 degrees for 40-50 minutes

Marinated Beans
Emmy Lou Dickinson, from My Cousin's Kitchen

16 oz wax beans
16 oz green beans
16 oz kidney beans
16 oz chick peas
2 large onions, thinly sliced

1 c vinegar
⅔ c salad oil
2 t salt
1 t pepper
1¼ c sugar

Combine drained vegetables and onions. Blend all other ingredients and bring to a boil. Cool slightly and pour over vegetables. Marinate in refrigerator overnight.

French Style Green Beans . . . an old standard
Lelia Ganter Handy

2 cans French style green beans
1 can mushroom soup
⅔ c milk

1 c grated cheddar cheese
1 can fried onion rings

Grease a 2 qt casserole, sprinkle grated cheese over drained beans in dish. Mix soup and milk and pour over mixture. Salt and pepper. Bake at 350 degrees for 25 minutes. Take from oven and top with a can of fried onion rings. Warm 5 more minutes.

Green Bean Casserole
Kim Overstreet

2 T butter
2 T flour
1 t salt
1 t sugar
1 T diced dried onions

1 can cream of mushroom soup
3 15-oz cans French style green beans
2 c shredded Swiss cheese
1 small can fried onion rings

Combine butter and flour, and cook gently. Remove from heat. Stir in salt, sugar, onions and cream of mushroom soup. Stir in beans. Place in shallow 2-quart casserole dish. Top beans with cheese and then onion rings. Bake for 30 minutes or until cheese is bubbling.

Barbequed Green Beans . . . but good
LaVece Hughes

1 16-oz can green beans
1 large onion, diced
3 slices bacon, cut up

½ c ketchup
¼ c vinegar
½ c sugar

Brown bacon and onions. Add ketchup, vinegar and sugar. Simmer until slightly thick. Drain beans and put in casserole dish. Pour sauce over beans. Mix and bake at 325 degrees about 30 minutes.

Green Bean and Corn Casserole
Janice Green

14¼-oz can French style green beans
11-oz can Green Giant white
   Shoepeg corn

1 c shredded cheddar cheese
½ c sour cream
buttered crushed Ritz crackers

Drain beans and corn. Add cheese and sour cream. Place in baking dish. Top with Ritz cracker crumbs and bake for 30-40 minutes.

Sometimes the heart sees what is invisible to the eye.
— H. Jackson Brown

Green Beans ... the country way
Tina Stevenson

1 country ham hock
2 slices Hickory flavored bacon,
      chopped
1 T bacon grease

50 oz can of green beans, drained
½ large onion, diced
heaping t of lemon pepper

Cook ham hock, bacon, onion and lemon pepper in large pot filled half way with water. "Boil down" until meat and onions are tender. Drain the water from the green beans and add to pot. Add enough water to cover. Cook for about 45 minutes. Add bacon grease during the last 15 minutes.

White Bean and Ham Soup
LaVece Hughes

2 c white beans
3 c water
1 t thyme
½ t pepper
1 medium onion

5 c chicken broth
½ c country ham, chopped
½ t marjoram
¼ t sage

Boil beans for 15 minutes in water. Cover and let stand for 1 hour. Then drain and add broth, 3 cups water, ham, thyme, marjoram, pepper and sage. Bring to boil. Reduce heat, simmer 2 hours. Add onion, and simmer 1 more hour.

"This is a yummy...great winter, weekend soup." — lgh

Pizza Carrots
Ann Burns

Peel and cook carrots; drain. Add 2 tablespoons butter, and ¼ cup ketchup; good shake of oregano, and garlic salt. Cook a little longer to warm everything.

The train of failure usually runs on the track of laziness.

Carrot Soufflé
Dee Harmon

1 pound carrots, cut into
    half-inch chunks
½ c melted butter
3 eggs

¼ c sugar
3 T flour
1 t baking powder
1 t vanilla

Cook carrots in pan of water for 15 minutes. Puree all of remaining ingredients and then add drained carrots and puree. Place in 8 inch greased casserole dish and cook for 45 minutes at 350 degrees. Serves six.

Topping:
½ c walnuts
⅓ c sugar
¼ c butter

Place on top of soufflé and bake 5-10 minutes more.

Glazed Carrots
Liz Woodward

2 bags frozen carrots (crinkle cut
    or baby size)
⅔ c margarine

dash salt
1½ c sugar (to taste)
dash of ginger

Drain carrots and barely cover with water in large pan. Add margarine, salt and sugar. Bring to boil and then turn down to simmer, for an hour if possible; if short on time, turn up heat but watch and stir often. Add ginger.

Glazed Baby Carrots
LaVece Hughes

1pkg (1 oz) Hidden Valley Ranch Dressing Mix
1pkg (16 oz) ready-to-eat baby carrots, cooked (boiled or steamed)
¼ cup light brown sugar
¼ cup butter

Melt butter and sugar in large skillet. Add carrots and dressing mix. Cook over medium heat until hot and glazed about 5 minutes. Serves four to six.

Carrot Copper Coins
Emmy Lou Miller Dickinson

2 lb sliced carrots,
    cut crosswise
1 green pepper, chopped
1 onion, thinly sliced
1 can tomato soup
½ c salad oil

1 c sugar
¾ c vinegar
1 t prepared mustard
1 t Worcestershire sauce
1 t salt
1 t pepper

Cook carrots until slightly tender. Drain well. Cool. Add onion and green pepper. Mix remaining ingredients and pour over carrot mixture. Marinate overnight in the refrigerator. Will keep 2 to 3 weeks.

Carrot Soup for Four
LaVece Hughes

4 c chicken broth
½ c whipping cream

4 large carrots, cut into chunks
2 T sugar

Bring broth and carrots to boil. Reduce and simmer until carrots are tender (about 15 minutes). Cool slightly, and process in small batches in blender until smooth. Return to pan and add cream and sugar.

Lima Beans Supreme
LaVece Hughes

1 box frozen Fordhook limas
1 small carton whipping cream
1½ t butter

½ t sugar
dash of salt
1 T cornstarch

Cook limas according to pkg directions, adding 1 t butter. Drain. Pour in whipping cream until it comes to the top of limas. Add ½ t butter, sugar and salt. Cook on low heat. Remove enough whipping cream from limas to make a thickening. Add cornstarch to the cream and mix well until smooth. Pour back into limas until they are slightly thickened and smooth.

Frozen Pea Casserole . . . very good
LaVece Hughes

2 10-oz boxes Frozen peas
1 small jar sliced water chestnuts
1 stick margarine melted

1 pkg Good Seasons Italian Dressing Mix (dry)
1 small can sliced mushrooms, drained

Mix and place all ingredients into a greased baking dish. Bake for 1 hour at 350 degrees covered with foil.

My family really likes this way to serve frozen peas.

Mashed Potatoes . . . you can make ahead
LaVece Hughes

5 lbs peeled potatoes
8 oz lite cream cheese
1 c sour cream
½ c butter

1 t onion salt
1 t seasoned salt
milk to thin

Cook potatoes until tender and drain. Beat softened cream cheese with half and half in mixer. Add hot potatoes and blend well. Add butter and seasonings. (Add milk if needed to thin down.) Put in 2-quart casserole. Brush top with butter and sprinkle on paprika. Bake in oven at 350 degrees for 30 minutes. Can be prepared ahead and refrigerated. Just bake longer to heat and brown.

Finally mashed potatoes that are really yummy and can be made ahead of time, if you can keep the family from eating them. Put them in the crock-pot on low to keep them warm until dinnertime.

Baked Potatoes . . . for the campfire
Chip Hughes and Charlie Dickinson, Boy Scout Camp on Skaggs Creek

1 sack of potatoes, or however many you want to eat, and several hands-full of fresh river mud. Let campfire burn down to red-hot coals. Pack potatoes individually in mud about ½ inch thick around potatoes. Place mud-wrapped potatoes in coals for about 30 minutes until mud is rock hard. Remove from coals and crack off mud.

Sweet and Sour Potatoes
LaVece Hughes

6-8 new potatoes, cubed and
  boiled in skins
1 medium onion, diced
¼ t salt

¼ t pepper
¾ c sugar
4 slices bacon, cut up
½ c vinegar

Boil potatoes and drain. Combine diced onion, salt, pepper and sugar. Add to potatoes. Cover. In a small frying pan, fry bacon until crisp. Add the vinegar to the hot bacon and bring to a boil. Pour immediately over the potato mixture. Mix well. Makes four to six servings.

Mushroom Soup
LaVece Hughes

2½ cups fresh mushrooms,
  chopped. (Shitake, if possible)
¼ c chopped onion
5 c chicken stock
4 T butter

⅓ c flour
1 c light cream
salt and pepper, to taste
¼ c sweet wine

Place the mushrooms and onion in the stock and simmer for 20 minutes. Work the butter and flour together to make a paste, then whisk this into the soup to thicken it. Stir in the cream. Salt and pepper to taste. Add the wine just before serving. Makes four servings.

Hash Brown Potato Casserole
LaVece Hughes

½ c melted butter
2¼ T minced onions
1 can cream of chicken soup
2 c grated sharp cheese
1 t salt

pepper
1 pt sour cream
2 lb frozen hash browns
½ c margarine
1 sleeve Ritz crackers

Thaw potatoes. Combine all ingredients except hash browns, Ritz crackers and ½ cup margarine. Add hash browns and mix well. Place in greased casserole. Mix Ritz and butter and sprinkle on top. Bake for 30 minutes at 375 degrees.

Fantastic Potato Soup
Janice Underwood

5 lb potatoes, cubed, cooked
    and drained
½ T butter
2 8-oz pkgs cream cheese
2 cans mushroom soup

dash garlic salt
2 c milk
2 cans cream of celery soup
diced onion
salt and pepper

Warm and serve with bacon pieces, parsley, and cheddar cheese on top.

Can serve this with buttered croissants. My family loves this soup. — lgh

Spinach Bisque
LaVece Hughes

3 5-oz pkgs frozen chopped spinach,
    thawed and well drained
3 c half and half cream
2 8-oz pkgs cream cheese
14½-oz can chicken broth

¾ c parmesan cheese
1 c shredded cheddar cheese
2 Garlic cloves
1 t salt
½ t pepper

In large pot, combine spinach and cream. Cover and cook over medium-low heat until heated through. Add remaining ingredients. Cook, uncovered, stirring constantly, until cheese is melted and soup is heated through. Serves twelve.

Baked Green Tomatoes
LaVece Hughes

5-6 green tomatoes
6 T butter
3 slices bread, finely chipped
1 t oregano
½ t thyme

½ t basil
½ t garlic
½ t sugar
⅓ c Parmesan cheese
salt and pepper

Lightly grease baking dish. Slice tomatoes ½ inch. Layer in dish, sprinkle sugar and salt and pepper. In saucepan brown bread crumbs and spices in 3 T butter. Sprinkle on top of tomatoes. Sprinkle cheese and dot with remaining 3 T butter. Bake for 45 minutes at 350 degrees.

Fried Green Tomatoes
LaVece Hughes

4 medium green tomatoes
1 c Aunt Jemima's cornmeal mix
⅓ t salt

½ t dried oregano or ½ t dried basil
bacon drippings or olive oil for frying
¼ t pepper

Cut tomatoes into ¼ inch slices, discarding top and bottom slice. Mix cornmeal mix with seasonings. Coat tomatoes well. In hot skillet containing bacon drippings or olive oil, add tomatoes slices in one layer. Lower heat to medium and fry for about 4 minutes or until golden brown. Serve with Parmesan cheese.

Tomato Soup
Ruth Landrum

10¾ oz Campbell's tomato
   bisque soup
14½ oz Red Gold tomatoes,
   diced with juice
14 oz half and half cream
¼ t garlic

1 t dill weed
3-4 drops Tabasco sauce
1 T butter
2-3 T Parmesan cheese
salt and pepper to taste

Mix all ingredients together and heat to boiling point, but do not boil. Let stand 10 minutes before serving. Serves four.

Breaded Tomatoes
LaVece Hughes

½ c chopped onion
2 T butter or margarine
2 T flour
2 14½-oz cans diced
   tomatoes, un-drained

½ c sugar
½ c oil
t salt
¼ t pepper
3 slices bread, toasted and cut
   into ¼-inch croutons

In a large saucepan, sauté onion in butter until tender; stir in flour until blended. Add the tomatoes, sugar, oil, salt and pepper. Bring to a boil; cook and stir for 2 minutes or until slightly thickened. Stir in croutons.

Colorful Vegetables
LaVece Hughes

1⅓ c (15 oz) green beans
1 medium green pepper, chopped
1 can tomatoes, chopped
1½ cups shredded cheddar cheese
½ c milk

1½ c chopped zucchini
½ c biscuit / baking mix
½ t pepper
½ t salt
3 eggs

Place beans and green peppers in a 13x9 baking dish. Top with tomatoes, cheese and zucchini. In a bowl combine the biscuit mix, salt, peppers, eggs and milk just until moistened. Pour over vegetables. Bake uncovered at 350 degrees for 55-60 minutes or until puffed and a knife inserted near the center comes out clean. Let stand for 10 minutes before serving. Serves six. Double for a crowd.

Vegetables and Stuffing
LaVece Hughes

¾ c mayonnaise
½ c milk
1 pkg (16 oz) stove top stuffing

1 pkg (16 oz) frozen broccoli,
chopped or vegetable blend
with broccoli, thawed

Mix dressing, milk and contents of vegetable seasoning packet from stuffing mix. Stir in stuffing crumbs, vegetable and cheese; toss to coat. Spoon into 11x7 baking dish. Bake 350 degrees for 20-25 minutes or until thoroughly heated. Serves six.

Can add 2 cups turkey or chicken for an easy one-dish meal.

Live to the point of tears.
-- Camus

Garden Vegetables and Bacon . . . yummy

LaVece Hughes

6 slices bacon
4 large potatoes (chopped and
    boiled)
1 to 2 banana peppers, or a
    small onion, chopped

4 tomatoes (diced) or 1 14-oz
    can with juice
6 eggs
salt and pepper to taste

Cook bacon until crisp in large skillet. Remove from skillet. When cool, break into pieces. Add potatoes to grease in skillet. Add peppers or onions, tomatoes, and bacon pieces. Beat eggs, and pour on top of potato mixture. Cook 15 minutes on medium heat until heated through and eggs are done. Salt and pepper to taste.

Meats

Apple Beef Stew
LaVece Hughes

2 pounds boneless chuck roast,
    cut into one- to half-inch cubes
2 T butter
2 medium onions, cut into wedges
2 T flour
⅛ t salt
2 cups water

2 T apple juice
2 bay leaves
½ t allspice
½ t cloves
2 medium carrots, sliced
2 medium apples, peeled and
    cut into wedges

In a large pot over medium heat, brown beef in butter. Add onions; cook until lightly browned. Sprinkle with flour and salt. Gradually add water and apple juice. Bring to a boil; cook and stir for 2 minutes. Add allspice, cloves, and bay leaf. Reduce heat; cover and simmer for 1 ½ hours or until meal is almost tender. Add carrots and apples; cover and simmer 15 minutes longer or until meat, carrots and apples are tender. Discard bay leaf. Serves four.

Boy Scout Mulligan . . . serves ten hungry scouts
LaVece Hughes

2½ lb hamburger
1 c water
1 lb elbow macaroni
¼ t salt

1 large onion
3 cans tomato soup
1 t sugar

Brown hamburger and onions in a pot over an open fire (*or on the stove, if you aren't a Boy Scout.*) Add rest of ingredients. Simmer until thickened.

"If I'm dead, I would like my epitaph to read, 'Curiosity, did kill this cat." — Studs Terkel

Cheeseburger Pie

LaVece Hughes

1 lb ground beef	1 c shredded Cheddar cheese
1 c chopped onion	1 ½ c milk
½ t salt	¾ c Bisquick baking mix
¼ t pepper	3 eggs

Heat oven to 400 degrees. Lightly grease 10-inch pie plate. Cook and stir beef and onion until brown; drain well. Stir in salt and pepper. Spread beef in pie plate; sprinkle with cheese. Beat remaining ingredients until smooth. Pour into pie plate. Bake until golden brown and knife inserted in center come out clean, about 30 minutes. Let stand 5 minutes. Serves six to eight.

Easy Chicken Casserole

LaVece Hughes

chicken or turkey, cooked and sliced or diced	1 can cream of chicken soup
1 pkg stuffing mix	1 can cream of celery soup
	8 oz sour cream

Cook chicken or turkey; cool and slice or dice. Prepare dressing according to packaged instructions. Place dressing in baking dish and layer chicken or turkey on top. Mix soups and sour cream and pour over top of chicken or turkey. Cover with aluminum foil and bake 30 minutes at 375 degrees. Remove foil and bake 10 minutes until golden brown.

In 1952, Albert Einstein, father of the Theory of Relativity, was offered the job of Prime Minister of Israel. Einstein, a pacifist, had worked for a homeland state for the Jews before WWII, but turned down the job of Prime Minister.

BBQ Chicken
Evelyn Barton, from Lelia Ann Dickinson Smith

2 or 2½ cut-up chickens
3 T catsup
2 T vinegar
2 T Worcestershire sauce
4 T water
2 T butter

3 T brown sugar
1 t salt
1 t mustard
1 t paprika
½ t cayenne pepper
1 t chili powder

Mix ingredients, heat to blend. Make folds in heavy-duty foil. Place foil on greased cookie sheet. Set oven for 500 degrees. Dip chicken pieces into sauce, place on foil, and pour remaining over chicken. Carefully fold in drugstore wrap. Cook 15 minutes at 500 degrees reduce temperature to 350 degrees for 1 hour and 15 minutes. **Do not open until ready to serve.**

Baked Chicken Poupon
LaVece Hughes

4 t Grey Poupon Dijon mustard
2 t water or oil
½ t Italian seasoning

1 t garlic powder
1 lb boneless chicken breast

Mix Grey Poupon, oil, garlic, Italian seasoning in large bowl or bag. Add chicken to coat. Bake 375 degrees for 20 minutes. Serve over wild rice. Serves four.

Chicken or Turkey Casserole
Betty Parker

2 c chunk chicken or turkey
1½ c uncooked noodle
1¾ c grated cheese
¼ green pepper, chopped,
    optional

½ small chopped onion
⅓ c diced pimentos
1 can undiluted mushroom soup
salt and pepper to taste

Cook, wash and drain noodles. Gently mix all ingredients together saving ¾ cup cheese for the topping. Place in casserole dish and bake at 350 degrees for 45 minutes or until slightly browned. Serves six.

Chicken Salad . . . great for a summer day
Susan Spears Hughes

8 oz boneless skinned chicken
    breast, cooked and cubed
3 stalks celery, sliced
1¼ c cooked long grain rice
1 c mayonnaise

2 T honey mustard
½ c green onions, chopped
½ c toasted slivered almonds
lemon pepper and dill weed
    to taste

Combine and chill.

Chinese Chicken Salad
Billie Neal Dickinson

4½ c cubed cooked chicken
1 small can water chestnuts,
    drained and sliced
1 c Mandarin oranges,
    drained

1 c diced celery
1 large can tidbit pineapple,
    drained
¼ c chopped green pepper
½ c sliced green olives

Mix all the above and add dressing. Refrigerate overnight.

Dressing:
½ pt mayonnaise   2 T grated mild onion
½ T prepared mustard

Before serving add 1 pkg dried hard Ramen noodles and slivered almonds.
Serve on a bed of lettuce.

When I first started to cook, my friend, Ann Burns, told me to always drain green beans to get rid of that "can" taste. She was right. — lgh

Indian Chicken Curry
Aunt Mildred Dickinson

½ c finely chopped onion
½ c finely chopped celery
¼ c butter
⅓ c flour
2 c chicken broth
1 c tomato juice

½ t Worcestershire sauce
1 T curry powder or more,
    according to taste
salt and pepper to taste
4 c diced, cooked chicken
4 c hot cooked rice

Lightly brown onion and celery in butter. Add flour and blend. Add broth, cook until thick, stirring constantly. Add tomato juice, Worcestershire sauce, seasonings and chicken. Heat thoroughly. Serve over cooked rice with the following condiments:

Coconut, shredded
Bacon, fried and crumbled
pecans or peanuts, chopped

chopped egg and yolk
chutney, "I like Major Greys'"

My Aunt Selma also used this recipe except that she used 1-cup tomato soup instead of tomato juice and 1 T curry powder. She also added the condiments of cashews, chopped apples, almonds, green peppers and onions. — lgh

Chicken Divan
Sondra Bowman Dickinson

2 10-oz pkg frozen broccoli
¼ c butter
¼ c flour
2 c chicken broth
½ c whipping cream

3 T cooking sherry
¼ t salt
¼ c Parmesan cheese
2 chicken breasts cooked and
    thinly sliced

Cook broccoli in boiling water and drain. Melt butter, blend in flour and add chicken broth. Cook and stir till thick: Stir in cream, sherry, salt, and dash pepper. Place broccoli in 13 x 9 x 2 Pyrex dish. Pour half of the sauce over, top with chicken slices. To remaining sauce add Parmesan cheese pour over chicken. Sprinkle with extra Parmesan cheese. Bake at 350 degrees for 20 minutes or till heated thoroughly. Place under broiler until sauce is golden. Careful not to burn. Serves six to eight.

"If you should die before me, ask if you can bring a friend."
— Stone Temple Pilots

Chicken Enchiladas
Joan Dickinson Walker

1 medium onion, chopped
1 clove garlic, crushed
1 T oil
3 T flour
1 can chicken broth + ½ can water
½ lb grated cheddar or
    Monterey Jack cheese

12 corn tortillas
1 lb boneless chicken breasts,
    cooked ("I microwave them")
½ c low fat sour cream or
    plain yogurt
½ t cumin
1 t chili powder

Sauté onion and garlic in oil until translucent. Gradually add flour and cook and stir a few minutes. Add spices and broth and water. Simmer about 10 minutes. Meanwhile cut up cooked chicken into bite size pieces. Add sour cream, a handful of the grated cheese and ⅓ cup of the sauce. Soften the tortillas in the microwave for 45 seconds to 1 minute on high. Put a few tablespoons of chicken mixture in each and roll up. Put a small amount of the sauce into the bottom of an ovenproof dish. (I use a large, rectangular, Pyrex dish). Place the filled tortillas in the dish. Top with remaining sauce and sprinkle the grated Cheese over that. Bake at 350 degrees for 20-25 minutes until cheese melts and sauce is bubbly.

"Lately I use 1 pound ground turkey instead of the chicken breasts (which I guess makes them Turkey Enchiladas). I cook the turkey, broken up, in a skillet and drain, then add in place of chicken."

Chicken Kabobs
Lucy White Carlson

4 whole boneless breasts of chicken, cubed
¼ c dry vermouth (or I sometimes use a dry white wine)

¼ c soy sauce
¼ c oil
1 clove garlic (crushed)

½ c pineapple juice
¼ t ginger
1 T honey

Marinate the chicken in a bowl with other ingredients for 2 to 3 hours. Skewer with green pepper, tomato, onion, pineapple. Grill, turning frequently and basting and with marinate.

Fried Chicken
Patsy Bergeon

Cut up chicken. Place several pieces in a pot, and sprinkle with salt and vinegar. Cover with lukewarm water: let stand for about 30 minutes. Drain. Combine self-rising flour with salt, garlic powder and black pepper. Melt solid vegetable shortening in a black iron skillet. You should have about 1 inch hot grease. Place chicken into hot grease. As it cooks, "tickle" the chicken. Gently move it around with a vegetable lifter. If you have enough grease, you won't have to turn it. Listen to the chicken. "When it gets quiet it's ready to come up," she said. When golden brown, about 20 minutes, lift from grease and drain on racks.

This special recipe comes from Patsy Robinson Bergeon, Paris, KY. Where folks know her for making the best-fried chicken in town. Miss Patsy finally gave the recipe to the Lexington Herald-Leader *when she decided "She couldn't take her secrets with her."*

Chicken-Country Ham Casserole
Selma Goodman Dickinson from Jane S. Goodman

3-4 whole chicken breasts,
   skinned and boned
½ c sherry
1 5-oz can sliced mushrooms,
   drained

½ c melted margarine
10¾ oz can mushroom soup
salt and paprika to taste

Sprinkle chicken with salt and paprika. Place ham slices in shallow dish. Top with chicken. "Sort of" wrap chicken with ham. Combine remaining ingredients and blend well. Pour over chicken. Bake 350 degrees for 1-1½ hrs. Yields six to eight servings.

Chicken Pot Pie . . . easy and very good
Ed Hughes

2 uncooked pie shells
5 chicken strips, sautéed; or
   2 skinless boneless breasts,
   cooked and cubed

1 small can peas
1 or 2 cans cream of chicken soup
1 or 2 potatoes, sliced
2 carrots, peeled and sliced

Mix chicken with peas and soup. Boil carrots and potatoes until half done. Pour chicken mixture into pie shell. Cover with potatoes and carrots. Cover with second shell. Cook for 45 minutes at 375 degrees.

Chicken Pot Pie . . . the easy way

LaVece Hughes

1 pkg stuffing mix
    for chicken
2 c cubed cooked chicken
1½ cups hot water
¼ c margarine, cut into pieces

¼ t dried thyme
12-oz jar of chicken gravy
10-oz frozen mixed
    vegetables, thawed, drained

Mix contents of vegetable/seasoning packet, hot water and butter in large bowl until butter is melted. Stir in stuffing crumbs just to moisten. Let stand about 5 minutes.
Mix chicken, gravy, vegetable and thyme in a 2 qt casserole. Spoon stuffing evenly over chicken mixture. Bake for 45 minutes at 350 degrees. Serves six.

Chicken Stuffing Casserole

LaVece Hughes

4 boneless chicken breasts,
    or 8 halves
1 can cream of mushroom soup

8 oz cheddar cheese, shredded
⅓ c white wine
2 cups herb stuffing mix
⅓ c butter

Spray Pyrex dish with Pam. Place chicken breast in glass baking dish. Cover with c of cheese. Mix soup and wine together and pour over chicken. Cover with stuffing and drizzle butter over the top. Bake at 350 degrees for 50 minutes.

Hawaiian Chicken

LaVece Hughes

1 chicken, or boneless turkey
    breast, cut up

Mix together:
1 jar apricot preserves
1 bottle Russian dressing
1 pkg onion soup mix

Dip chicken pieces in mixture, covering each piece well. Place in large Pyrex baking dish and spoon leftover mixture on each piece. Bake at 325 degrees for 1½ hours.

Baked Chili

LaVece Hughes

3 pkg chili-flavored ramen noodles
2 cans chili, with or without beans

10 oz bag plain corn chips
12 oz pkg cheddar cheese
Jalapeno slices, optional

In a large saucepan, prepare ramen noodles according to package directions. Add cans of chili and corn chips. Once mixed, pour in a cake pan or casserole dish. Sprinkle shredded cheese on top and place jalapeno slices if desired on top. Bake in a 350 degree oven for about 20 minutes or until cheese is evenly melted.

White Chili . . . really good

Chris Howard Dickinson

1 lb large white beans
6 c chicken broth
2 cloves garlic, minced
2 medium onions, chopped
2 T oil
2 4-oz cans mild green
    chilics, chopped
Salsa, sour cream and corn chips

2 t ground cumin
1½ t oregano
¼ t ground clove
¼ t cayenne pepper
4 c cooked chicken breast,
    diced
3 c Monterey Jack cheese

Combine beans, broth, garlic and half the onions in a large soup pot. Bring to a boil. Reduce heat, simmer until beans are soft (3 hrs or more) adding more broth or water if necessary. In a skillet, sauté remaining onions in oil until tender. Add chilies and season and mix thoroughly. Add to bean mixture. Add chicken and simmer 1 hour. Serve topped with grated cheese, salsa, and sour cream and with chips on the side. Serves eight to ten.

> *"You don't have to practice every day, only on the days you eat!*
> *— Suzuki*

> *If you live to be a hundred, I want to live to be a 100, minus 1 day,*
> *so that I won't have to live without you. — Winnie the Pooh*

Chicken with Apple Cream Sauce

Victoria Casey

4 boneless skinless chicken
    breast halves
1 T oil
1 c apple juice
1 t lemon juice
½ t dried rosemary, crushed

½ t salt
⅛ t pepper
1 T cornstarch
½ c whipping cream
1 t dried parsley flakes
1 pkg Uncle Ben's Wild Rice

In a skillet over medium heat, cook the chicken in oil for 4 minutes on each side or until browned. Combine the apple juice, lemon juice, rosemary, salt and pepper; pour over chicken. Reduce heat; cover and simmer for 10 minutes or until chicken juices run clear. Remove chicken and keep warm. Combine cornstarch and cream until smooth; stir into cooking liquid in skillet. Bring to a boil; cook and stir for 2 minutes or until thickened. Add parsley. Return chicken to skillet and heat through. Serve over rice. Serves four.

Cousin Hillary Clinton's Chicken & Rice

LaVece Hughes

2 T chopped onion
2 T chopped green pepper
2 T butter
2 c cooked chicken, chopped
    into bite-size pieces
6-oz pkg wild rice or long
    grain and wild rice, cooked

1 can French-style green beans, drained
1 can cream of celery or chicken soup
1 c grated cheddar cheese
juice of a lemon
½ c sliced water chestnuts
salt and pepper to taste
½ c mayonnaise

Sauté the onion and green pepper in butter. Combine all ingredients except the cheese and place in a greased 2 qt casserole dish. Bake uncovered for 25-30 minutes at 350 degrees. Top with cheese and cook 5 minutes more.

This cousin makes a really good chicken and rice casserole.

Chicken Roll-Ups
Liz Woodward

8 chicken breasts   1 slice luncheon ham
8 slices mozzarella

Flatten chickens breasts with meat tenderizer. Roll together with chicken on outside– ham, cheese and chicken. Hold together with toothpicks. Brown roll-ups in skillet.

Mix and pour over chicken:
    1 can cream of chicken soup
    ⅓ c of white wine

Bake at 350 degrees until thoroughly heated..

Hot Chicken Salad . . . a family favorite
Kate Dickinson Ganter

3 c cooked cubed chicken
1½ c chopped celery
¾ c almond slivers
6 oz sliced water chestnuts
½ t salt
2 t grated onion

3 T lemon juice
1 can cream of chicken soup
1½ c mayonnaise
¾ c sharp cheddar, grated
1½ c crushed Chinese noodles

Combine everything but the cheese and potato chips in a greased 9 X 13 inch casserole. Combine the cheese and noodles and sprinkle on top. Bake in a preheated 325 degree oven for 45 minutes or until lightly browned. Serves eight.

"Friends love you for who you are, and in spite of who you are."
— Rev. Bill McDonald

Cowboy Beans
J. Brandon Price

3 16-oz cans of pork and beans
24-oz can of chili beans
1 medium to large onion, chopped
1 green pepper, chopped

1 jar of mushrooms
1 lb hamburger
16 oz ketchup
¾ lb brown sugar

Brown hamburger in a skillet with chopped onion and green pepper. Drain the grease. Place the remaining ingredients and beef mixture into a 5 qt crock-pot and cook on low for 8 hours without a top. Do not stir the mixture during cooking; it's maintenance free.

Dinner in a Dish
Chip Hughes

4 T butter
2 medium onions, chopped
2 green peppers, diced, optional
1 can tomatoes, sliced
1 lb ground beef
1½ t salt

¼ t pepper
2 eggs
2 c corn, fresh or canned
1 c dry breadcrumbs
 butter

Put butter in skillet and lightly fry onion and peppers for 3 minutes. Add seasonings. Remove from heat and stir in eggs and mix well. Put 1 cup corn in baking dish (1½ quart), then half the meat mixture, then a layer of sliced tomatoes, and another layer of corn, then meat and then tomatoes. Pour juice from tomatoes over top. Cover with crumbs and dot generously with butter. Bake in moderate oven, about 350 degrees, for 35 minutes. Serves six.

May use fresh tomatoes, but should add a little ketchup and water to casserole.

"Friends are siblings, God never gave us!" — Chastity Ross

Pickled Eggs
Myrtle Webb

3½ c white vinegar
2 c water
½ c sugar
1 onion, sliced and
    separated into rings

2 cloves garlic
4 bay leaves
2 dozen hard-boiled eggs, shelled
4 t salt

In a saucepan, Bring to a boil. Simmer 30 minutes. Cool. Add beets and juice and onions combine vinegar, water, sugar, salt, celery seed, garlic and bay leaves.. Pour over eggs in crock, jar or bowl. Cover and refrigerate at least a week. The eggs improve with age and will last for months if kept in a glass jar with a tight lid. It you want white eggs leave out the beets.

Mrs. Webb is a teacher and she created this recipe to take eggs to her classroom when the class studied pioneer days. lgh

Delicious Fish in Herb Butter
Sandy Godecker

1 lb fresh fish (I use Orange Roughy)
½ t basil
½ c margarine
⅔ c crushed saltine crackers
¼ c Parmesan cheese

½ t oregano
½ t salt
¼ t garlic powder

Mix together crumbs and seasonings in a plastic bag. Melt butter in oven in 13 x 9 pan. Dip fish in butter and then in seasoning. Shake, and then put back in pan. Bake 25-30 minutes at 350 degrees. May need to turn on broiler last couple of minutes just to brown slightly.

"Hello, Grandma? Mama has gone to the hospital and Bobby,
Mary Kate, Daddy and I are here at home all alone!"
Rev. Bill McDonald, Mother's Day Sermon

Fish Cakes

Billa Coy from Mildred Maupin

4 c cooked fish (your choice)
2 c mashed potatoes
1 egg
salt and pepper to taste

1 onion, chopped
parsley flakes
Parmesan cheese
cracker crumbs

Mix all ingredients well, adding more cracker crumbs to desired consistency and roll into patties. Refrigerate if time permits. Brown on both sides in a skillet with oil.

Can use canned salmon and can be frozen to add extra crunch, coat them in cornmeal before frying. — lgh

Fish Chowder, Boston Style

LaVece Hughes

3 slices bacon
½ c chopped celery
½ c chopped onion
1 clove garlic
¼ c flour
4 T flour
4 cups water

6 chicken bouillon cubes
1½ cups diced potatoes
1 lb white fish fillets, cut into
    bite-sized pieces
2 c light cream
2 T chopped pimentos

In a large Dutch oven, cook bacon until crisp; remove and crumble. In drippings cook celery, onion and garlic until tender. Stir in flour. Gradually add water and bouillon cubes, stirring until smooth. Bring to boil and add potatoes. Reduce heat and cool 10 minutes. Stir in fish and cook 15 minutes longer. Add cream and pimento, and heat. Garnish with bacon.

Golfer Gary Player said of his friend Jack Nicholas—
"He's the greatest loser in the history of golf.
Now that's the real mark of a champion!"

Gingersnap Stew
LaVece Hughes

3 carrots, cut into ¾-inch pieces
3 medium stalks celery,
    cut into half-inch pieces
¼ c chopped onion
2 t cooking oil
8 oz cooked smoked sausage,
    halved lengthwise and
    cut into 1-inch pieces

1½ cups water
½ of a 15-oz can kidney beans,
    rinsed and drained
1 T chili powder
1 T Worcestershire sauce
1 14-oz can stewed tomatoes
6 gingersnaps, crushed (about ⅓ cup)

In a large saucepan cook carrots, celery, and onion in hot oil over medium heat about 5 minutes or until onion is nearly tender. Remove vegetables from pan. Add sausage pieces to pan. Cook over medium heat until lightly browned. Return vegetables to pan. Add water, beans, chili powder, and Worcestershire sauce. Bring to boiling; reduce heat. Simmer, covered, about 20 minutes or until vegetables are tender. Stir in un-drained tomatoes. Add crushed gingersnaps. Cook and stir about 5 minutes. Ladle into bowls. Serves four

Green Bean Dinner . . . from Grandmother Ganter
Aaron M. Tilton

Cook a pot of potatoes and green beans. Use either fresh or canned green beans, but if canned pour off water from can and add fresh water to eliminate that canned taste. Add bacon, ham hock, or several tablespoons of bacon grease and potatoes to green beans and cook together until potatoes are done and beans are soft. Make "lace edged batty cakes," and slice fresh onions and tomatoes. Make a one-dish meal by allowing family to mix green beans and potatoes, onions and tomatoes cut up, corn bread torn in small pieces and pour "pot liquor" (juice) from beans over all. Add salt and pepper and enjoy.

A little boy came home from school, " Mommy, Mommy,
I got a part in the school play! I was chosen
to sit in the audience and clap."
— Rev. Larry Bishop

Stuffed Green Peppers
Lillian Stivers

2 onions, chopped
1 lb ground beef
1 large can tomato sauce

1½ c breadcrumbs
8 green peppers, hollowed
¼ lb Velveeta

Brown beef and onions in oil. Add tomatoes and breadcrumbs. Simmer. Parboil the peppers, drain. Cut Velveeta into small cubes, add to beef. Stuff peppers with beef. Heat until hot in 350-degree oven. Serves eight.

Cooking a Smoked Ham
Kate Dickinson Ganter

To cook a smoked ham, either whole or part, scrub clean, then place in a large pot. Cover with hot water having ½ c vinegar and ½-cup brown sugar dissolved in it. Bring to a boil then reduce heat and simmer for 20 to 25 minutes per pound. Allow to cool in this liquid (over night is OK), then remove from pot and take off skin. Make a paste of: ½ cup mustard, ¼ cup brown sugar, and 3 ounces thawed orange juice concentrate. Spread on ham and bake at 300 to 325 degrees for 30 minutes to 1 hour.

Raisin Sauce For Ham
LaVece Hughes

Mix:
½ c brown sugar
½ T mustard
½ T flour

Add:
¼ c vinegar
1¾ c water

Place in microwave for 2 minutes. Stir and cook 3 minutes more and add ½ cup raisins.

Country Ham

Selma Goodman Dickinson from Mary Mitchell

Scrub thoroughly. Soak at least 48 hours – changing water several times. On second day add 1 cup cider vinegar and 1 cup brown sugar. Scrub after 2 and 3 water changes. Line roaster pan with heavy-duty foil. Place ham fat side down. Add 6 orange slices and more brown sugar. Pour 1 cup Makers Mark over ham. Seal foil tightly around ham. Pour water ½ way up on side of ham. Place lid on roaster. Bake at 350 degrees for 18 minutes per pound.

Ham Pudding

Donna Fegenbush

Ritz crackers, crushed
1 c grated American cheese
small jar chopped pimento pepper
buttered Ritz cracker crumbs

1½ c of a thick white sauce
2 c chopped ham
4 hard-boiled eggs

In a shallow, buttered 9 x 9 baking dish, place a quarter inch layer of crushed cracker crumbs. Moisten well with about ½ to ¾ medium cup of thick cream sauce. Use half the ingredients for each of the following layers: add a layer of grated American cheese, a layer of chopped or finely-diced ham, and a layer of finely diced pimento followed by a layer of grated hard-boiled eggs. Sprinkle with pepper. Repeat layers to fill dish. Top with buttered crumbs. Bake in a 375-degree oven about 25 minutes or until bubbly hot and crusty. Makes six to eight servings.

Years ago, the story goes, President Dwight Eisenhower visited the birthplace of Abraham Lincoln at Hodgenville, Kentucky, where this recipe was served. The president asked for a second helping, also for a copy of the recipe to add to his collection.

The expression "rule of thumb" originates from an old law which stated that a man was allowed to beat his wife with a rod that was no larger than his thumb.
— Rev. Lisa W. Davison

Ham and Pasta Bake
Suzanne Brown

¼ c flour
1 T dried minced onion
1¼ t salt
½ t ground mustard
⅛ t pepper
2½ c milk
10 oz frozen chopped broccoli,
    cooked and drained
2 c elbow macaroni, cooked
    and drained

2 c cubed fully cooked ham
¾ c shredded cheddar cheese

Topping:
2 T margarine, melted
½ c Ritz crackers, crumbled,
    or dry bread crumbs

In a medium saucepan, combine the flour, onion, salt, mustard and pepper. Gradually stir in milk until blended. Bring to a boil; cook and stir for 2 minutes or until thickened and bubbly. Stir in broccoli, macaroni, ham and cheese. Transfer to an un-greased 2 quart baking dish. For topping, combine butter and crackers or dry breadcrumbs. Sprinkle over macaroni mixture. Bake uncovered at 350 degrees for 30 minutes or until golden brown.

Kids especially like this creamy creation.

Mama's Monday Night Hamburger Casserole
Lelia Ann Dickinson Smith

½ to 1 lb ground beef, cooked
    and drained. (Discard grease.)
1 small chopped onion
1 small can mushrooms or
    fresh mushrooms, sautéed
2 T flour
1 c macaroni, cooked

2 beef bullion cubes dissolved in
    2 c hot water
½ t soy sauce
½ bay leaf
3 T tomato paste
salt and pepper to taste

Sauté onions, mushrooms in olive oil until slightly browned. Add hamburger, which has been cooked and drained. Cover and simmer 10 minutes. Thicken with flour, add water with bullion cubes and cook until thickened, stirring. Add tomato paste, bay leaf, soy sauce, salt and pepper and cook a few minutes. Add cooked macaroni. Pour into casserole and cover with grated Parmesan cheese. Bake 350 degrees for 30 minutes.

Hamburger Bean Casserole
Charlie Hughes

1 lb ground beef
1 24-oz can baked beans
1 jar barbeque sauce

2 c shredded cheddar cheese
1 can Hungry Jack biscuits

Preheat oven to 400 degrees. Brown ground beef and drain grease. Add beans and barbeque sauce until desired flavor is reached. Pour into 13 x 9 inch pan. Cut biscuits in half and spread around corners of the pan. Add cheese on top. Cook in oven until biscuits are brown.

Hamburger Cornpone Pie
LaVece Hughes

1 lb hamburger
1 #2 can tomatoes
1 #2 can red kidney beans
1 c cornbread mix

2 medium onions, chopped
2 t chili powder
2 t Worcestershire sauce
salt & pepper to taste

Brown hamburger and onions. Pour off grease. Add chili powder, Worcestershire sauce, salt, pepper, and tomatoes. Cover pan and cook 15 minutes. Add beans; pour into greased 2 qt casserole. Cover with thin layer of corn bread batter. (Corn bread batter should be thinner than regular) Bake at 400 degrees for 25 to 30 minutes.

Stuffed Knockwurst & Potato Salad
LaVece Hughes

2 cans Read German potato
    salad plus 2 T vinegar
1½ lb knockwurst sausage

1 can sauerkraut, chopped & drained
4 slices Swiss cheese, cut into strips

Spread potato salad in a 12 x 7 baking dish. Slice knockwurst lengthwise so that it can be spread open and put sauerkraut on top of sausage. Top with cheese and embed it in the potato salad. Bake at 350 degrees for 25–30 minutes. Makes 6-8 servings

Hot Brown Sandwich

LaVece Hughes

Sauce:

2 T butter

¼ c flour

2 c milk

¼ t salt

½ t Worcestershire sauce

¼ c sharp cheddar cheese, grated

¼ c grated Parmesan cheese

Melt butter in a saucepan; add flour and stir well. Add milk, cheeses and seasonings, and cook, stirring constantly, until thick.

Sandwich:

½ lb turkey, sliced thin

8 slices trimmed toast

8 strips bacon, partially cooked

4 oz grated Parmesan cheese

½ lb ham, sliced thin

4 slices tomato

Cut toast into triangles and place on a baking sheet or Individual baking dishes. Arrange turkey and ham slices on the toast and cover with hot cheese sauce. Top with tomato slices and bacon strips. Sprinkle with Parmesan cheese. Bake at 425 until bubbly. Serves four.

This is similar to the popular "Hot Brown" which originated at the Brown Hotel in Louisville, in the late 1920's. I use more cheese.

King Solomon had a saying that would make those who felt bad, feel good, and those who felt good, feel bad. It was, "This, too, shall pass."

Microwave Meatloaf . . . 15 minutes, and great
LaVece Hughes

1 lb ground beef
1 egg
½ c bread crumbs
¼ c milk

2 t onion soup mix
2 T catsup
2 T Worcestershire sauce
½ c Swiss or cheddar cheese, shredded

Combine all ingredients and shape into a round or oval loaf. Squish with fingers of both hands to mix. Shake additional ketchup onto top of meatloaf and spread. Place in microwave-safe dish (preferably one which allows the grease to drain while cooking); cover dish with waxed paper. Microwave on high for 15 minutes or until done, turning dish after five minutes of cooking. Drain and cover with foil. Let stand before slicing. Yields four to six servings.

A quick way to have a really moist, yummy meatloaf for dinner.

Old Maid Stew
LaVece Hughes

1 lb ground beef, browned
1 medium onion
2 cloves garlic
16 oz can kidney beans, rinsed
16 oz can baked beans with liquid
15 oz can butter beans, rinsed
14 oz can beef broth
11 oz can corn with liquid

10½-oz can vegetable soup,
  undiluted
6-oz tomato paste
1 c sliced carrots
1 c sliced celery
2 T chili powder
1 t each, oregano, thyme, salt
½ t each, marjoram and pepper

Pour all ingredients into a crock-pot and mix well. Cook for about 4 hours.

Pork Chop Casserole
From Elizabeth Harlow and Selma Goodman Dickinson

1 can celery soup
1 can cream of mushroom soup
1 c uncooked rice

6-8 pork chops
1 c water, ¾ c water

Mix celery soup & mushroom soup. Put ½ of soup mix in bottom of a pan. Add 1 c uncooked rice, 1 c water. Brown 6 - 8 chops, and place them on top of rice. Pour remaining half of soup mixture over chops. Add ¾-cup water. Cover pan and bake at 350 degrees for 1½ hours.

Microwave Lasagna

Aaron Tilton

1½ t olive oil
½ pound ground beef
½ c grated Parmesan or
    Romano cheese
1 egg, slightly beaten
2 c ricotta cheese
2 t dried parsley flakes

1 32-oz jar spaghetti sauce
6 uncooked lasagna noodles
1½ c shredded mozzarella cheese
2 T shredded or grated
Parmesan or Romano cheese

Put olive oil and ground beef into a 9 inch glass pie plate. Cover with waxed paper. Cook in microwave oven 2 minutes on high, or until meat is no longer pink: Stir and break meat apart with a wooden spoon. Drain off fat from meat. Set aside.

Combine ½ cup Parmesan cheese, the egg, ricotta cheese and parsley flakes. Pour 1 c spaghetti sauce over bottom of a 1½ quart glass-baking dish. Put ⅓ of uncooked lasagna noodles (break to fit dish if necessary) in a layer on sauce. Layer with half each of mozzarella, cooked beef and cheese mixture. Repeat layers. Put remaining noodles over cheese mixture. Spread remaining sauce on top. Cover with waxed paper. Cook in microwave oven 12 minutes on high: rotate dish ¼ turn. Cook covered 20 minutes at medium or until noodles are done.

Remove dish from oven: cover with aluminum foil and let stand 20 minutes. Before serving, sprinkle remaining Parmesan cheese over to. Six servings

Ratatouille

Jeanne Dickinson White from Selma Goodman Dickinson

½ lb pork sausage (bulk)
1 garlic clove, crushed
2 c or ½ lb cubed eggplant
½ c green pepper, cut in
    half-inch pieces
¼ t pepper

¼ c thinly sliced onion
1 T flour
¾ c sliced zucchini (4 oz)
1 16-oz can tomatoes
½ t salt
½ t sweet basil

Cook pork sausage, onion and garlic until well done. Drain off fat. Stir in flour; add eggplant, zucchini, green pepper, tomatoes, and the liquid, salt, pepper, and basil. Stir, breaking up tomatoes. Cover and simmer 20 minutes, stirring occasionally.

St. Charles Spaghetti Sauce
Jeanne Dickinson White

1 lb spaghetti
2 cloves garlic
1 lb ground chuck
8-oz can tomato sauce
2 c tomato juice
6-oz can tomato paste
1 t dry parsley

1 med sized onion, chopped
3½ T olive oil
¾ t salt
¼ t pepper
¼ t basil
1 T sugar

Simmer onion and garlic in oil until soft. Drain. Brown meat and drain off fat. Add onion/garlic mixture to meat along with tomato juice, sauce, paste, spice and sugar. Simmer 2 ½ to 3 hours stirring occasionally. Cook spaghetti according to pkg. directions and serve with sauce.

Scalloped Oysters for Thanksgiving
Margaret Holman from Mildred Dickinson

1 pt fresh oysters
1½ c heavy cream
   or half and half
⅓ c butter

2½ c crushed soda crackers
6 drops Tabasco sauce
salt to taste
few grains cayenne pepper

Drain oysters. Line a shallow casserole with 1-cup crackers. Lay the drained oysters on the crackers sprinkle with salt and dot with butter. Cover oysters with remaining 1½ cups crackers. Mix Tabasco with cream and pour over all. The cream should barely cover the oysters, leaving a layer of crackers uncovered on top. Dot with remaining butter. Cook in preheated 425-degree oven for 20 to 30 minutes or until golden brown.

To give canned biscuits pizzazz, brush the tops with Italian salad dressing before baking. They taste like garlic bread. — lgh

Meatballs
Eula Spears

3 lbs ground beef
1 pkg Lipton onion soup mix
2 eggs

3 t seasoning salt
2 c seasoned breadcrumbs

Sauce:
2 jars currant jelly

28-oz bottle ketchup

Mix first 5 ingredients with hands. Shape into balls and bake on cookie sheet for 20 minutes at 350 degrees. Put in crock-pot with jelly and ketchup, simmer in sauce for 2 hours before eating.

Pork Roast . . . from Grandma Alley
Will Dickinson

3 to 4 lb pork loin rubbed with salt

Brown on top of stove in very, very hot, heavy roasting pan. It must be very brown—almost burned on all sides and ends. Roast in open pan at 325 degrees, 45 minutes per pound.

Gravy:
Pour off excess fat leaving brown juices in pan and approximately 3-4 tablespoons fat. Mix flour into fat and add water to make a thin paste (4 T flour, ½ c water) stirring constantly to keep smooth. Add water to desired consistency. Salt and pepper to taste. (Optional - add bay leaf) Gravy must be boiled in order to cook flour, therefore, the consistency will have to be adjusted with water.

Pork Chops . . . in sour cream sauce
LaVece Hughes

6 pork chops
¼ t salt
⅛ t pepper
¾ c beef broth
1 T barbeque sauce

⅓ c evaporated skim milk
⅓ c non-fat sour cream
3 T flour
chopped parsley

Sprinkle pork chops with salt and pepper. Spray large skillet with non-stick cooking spray. Heat over medium-high heat until hot. Add port chops; cover and cook 4-6 minutes or until golden brown, turning once.

In a small bowl, mix half cup of the broth and the barbeque sauce. Pour over port chops; cover tightly. Reduce heat to medium-low; simmer 5-10 minutes until pork is no longer pink in center. Remove pork chops from skillet; cover. In same small bowl, combine remaining ¼ cup broth, milk sour cream and flour; beat until smooth. Pour into same skillet; cook and stir over medium heat for 2 to 3 minutes or until bubbly and thickened. Serve over pork chops and sprinkle with parsley.

The Case of the Smothered Pork Chops
Maria Dickinson

4 thick pork chops
½ c uncooked rice
salt and pepper

1 lemon
1 can of golden mushroom soup
½ can of water

Heat oven to 325 degrees. Cut fat off the pork chops. Melt the fat in a skillet over low head. Put the chops in and brown on both sides. Pour rice into a baking dish and place the browned chops over the rice. Peel and cut the onion in to 4 slices and place one on each chop. Sprinkle with salt and pepper. Cut the lemon into 4 slices and set on top of the onion slices. Pour the mushroom soup and ½ can of water over the chops. Cover the dish. Bake for 1 hour.

"This recipe is taken from The Nancy Drew Cookbook. *The Nancy Drew Mystery Books were my favorite to read back when I was younger. However, I do still enjoy making this recipe for my family."*

Beef Stroganoff . . . mother's version
Mildred Dickinson

2 lb sirloin steak, cut in strips
½ c finely chopped onions
2 T butter
2 T flour
2 bouillon cubes dissolved
    in 1½ c boiling water

½ c sour cream
1 t dry mustard
1½ t salt and pepper
1 c or 4-oz can mushroom pieces
    with liquid
2 T tomato paste

Cook beef in butter until browned. Remove and add onion. Cook short time; blend in flour, brown and slowly add bouillon mixture. Cook until mixture thickens. Add tomato paste, seasonings and meat. Simmer until meat is tender, about 30 minutes. Fold in sour cream and heat thoroughly, do not boil. Serve over rice or noodles.

Beef Stroganoff . . . daughter's version
Ann Beal

1 to 1½ lbs sirloin tips
6 T butter
2 T chopped green onion
½ to 1 c sliced fresh mushrooms
½ c wine

Worcestershire sauce
1½ c sour cream
salt
pepper
chopped parsley

Chop onions, mushrooms, and parsley and set aside. Cut meat in thin strips. Melt 4 tablespoons of butter in a skillet and get it as hot as you can without burning. Add sirloin tips. When they are delicately brown on both sides and done (this takes only a minute or two) remove them to a platter. Add remaining butter and the chopped green onions and mushrooms and cook for a minute. Then add the wine, a dash or two of Worcestershire sauce, and the sour cream. Stir well and heat through, but do not boil or the sour cream will curdle. Salt to taste. Add the beef and parsley to the sauce, removing from the heat almost immediately. Top with freshly ground black pepper. Serve over rice. Serves four.

"This sauce take only a few minutes to prepare, once the meat has been sliced and the onions and mushrooms have been chopped."

Hamburger Stroganoff . . . grandsons' version
Aaron and Ike Walker

1 lb lean ground beef
1 medium onion, chopped
1 4-oz. can mushrooms
1 10½-oz can cream of
    mushroom soup

2 T ketchup
1 T Worcestershire sauce
1 c sour cream
salt, pepper to taste

Crumble beef in skillet and brown. Drain excess fat. Add onion and cook several minutes until translucent. Add mushrooms, soup, ketchup, and Worcestershire sauce. Cook and stir over medium heat for a few minutes so that it simmers. Reduce heat to low and stir in sour cream. Heat through but do not let it come to a simmer after sour cream is added. Serve over noodles.

Pork Chops with Apples and Stuffing
Joan Hamilton

6 boneless pork chops
1 T oil

6-oz pkg stuffing mix
21-oz apple pie filling with cinnamon

Brown pork chops in skillet in oil. Meanwhile, prepare stuffing mix according to pkg directions. Spread pie filling into a greased 13 x 9-baking dish. Place the pork chops on top; spoon stuffing over chops. Cover and bake for 35 minutes at 350 degrees. Uncover; bake 10 min longer.

Roast Beef . . . fantastic, family favorite
Kate Ganter

3 to 4 lb chuck roast
1 pkg onion soup mix
1 can cream of mushroom soup

Put large piece of aluminum foil in pan; spread half of dry soup mix in this. Lay roast on soup mix, sprinkle rest of mix on top. Pour undiluted soup mix over top. Seal all tightly in foil. Bake 2½ hours at 350 degrees. When finished, remove roast and pour gravy in a gravy dish.

"This recipe from my mother is one of my family's favorites, and may be cooked all day in the crock pot on low if need be." — lgh

Country Fried Steak
Charlie G. Hughes, Sr.

Cut round steak (cubed is best) into serving sized steaks. Flour on both sides and brown well in skillet of about 4 heaping tablespoons of melted shortening. Salt and pepper and set aside as browned. Pour off all but 2-3 T grease. To remaining grease in skillet add enough flour to absorb all the grease and stir over medium heat until brown. Add enough water to skillet to fill to about half full. Add enough Kitchen Bouquet to turn gravy to your favorite shade of brown. Add salt and pepper to taste. Allow gravy to boil for a minute or two, stirring as it boils. Place meat in heavy pan and cover with gravy. Cover and cook on burner over low heat for at least 2 hours. May cook in crock-pot on high for about 3 hours or may cook on low longer, or may cook in oven at 350 degrees for 2 to 3 hours.

Sauerkraut & Sausage Dinner
Pat Alexander Nielsen

1 pkg Kielbasa sausage	1 container sauerkraut
2 apples, Granny Smith or Gala	1 c wine
2 hands full of brown sugar	About 2 c water

Cut apples into slices; place everything in a large pot and boil on top of stove until apples and sausages are cooked, about 30 minutes

Pepper Steak
Pat Dickinson

3 c cooked rice	½ c sliced green onions
1 lb round steak	2 green peppers, cut in strips
1 T paprika	2 T cornstarch
2 T Butter or margarine	¼ c each water and soy sauce
2 cloves garlic, crushed	2 large tomatoes, cut in eighths
1½ c beef broth	

Pound steak to ¼ inch. Cut into strips. Sprinkle meat with paprika. Brown meat in butter. Add garlic and broth. Cover and simmer 30 minutes. Stir in onion and green pepper. Cover and cook 5 minutes more. Blend cornstarch, water and soy sauce. Stir into meat. Cook until clear and thick. Add tomatoes and stir gently. Serve over regular or fried rice.

Pig Picking for a Party . . . cooks eleven hours
Henry Walker

90-110 pound pig, dressed
Soaked hickory chips, nuts, and branches
50 lb charcoal plus lighter

Buy pig. Haul it home. Place pig on grill, skin side down.

Start 10 pounds charcoal. Once hot, shovel it under pig onto surface of bottom of cooker - about 2 feet from pig. Make sure charcoal is not directly under pig so that dripping fat misses most of the charcoal. Put more charcoal under thicker sections. Add chips to charcoal for hickory flavor. Add more as needed. Start and add second 10-pound charcoal about 2 hours later. Add more chips as needed. Every 1½ - 2 hours add 10 pounds of charcoal till 50 pounds is used.

Ready in about 11 hours of cooking. Pick it!

"I charge $5.00 an adult or teenager so that I can afford to do this".

Mexican Pork Chops and Beans
Janice Green

1 large (14 x 20) cooking bag	½ t garlic powder
2 T flour	4 pork chops
1 c thick and chunky salsa	1 16-oz can red kidney beans, drained
2 T lime juice	2 medium green, yellow, orange or red
¾ t chili powder	sweet peppers cut in cubes

Shake flour in cooking bag. Place in a 13 x 9 baking dish. Add salsa, lime juice, chili powder and garlic powder to bag. Squeeze bag to blend ingredients. Place pork chops in bag. Spoon beans and peppers around pork chops. Close bag with nylon tie; cut 6 half–inch slits in top. Bake at 350 degrees for 35-40 minutes. Let stand in bag 5 minutes.

"I was born modest, but it didn't last."
— Mark Twain

119

Ladies Special Sandwich
Mildred Dickinson

rye bread
lettuce leaves
sliced chicken or turkey

sliced tomato
thousand island dressing
bacon bits

For each serving butter a large slice of rye bread. Place butter side up on dinner plate. First put on several leaves of lettuce, then a layer of thin slices of Swiss cheese. Add lettuce leaf, cover with slices of white meat of chicken or turkey.
Pour Thousand Island Dressing over all. Top with tomato slice, then a hard cooked egg slice. Garnish with crisp hot bacon slices, ripe olives and parsley.

Thousand Island Dressing:
To one-cup mayonnaise add ½-cup chili sauce, 3 hard cooked eggs, chopped; small amount of chopped celery and green pepper, minced onion, if desired.

"This recipe doesn't sound like much trouble, but it is! I use it for my bridge club, it makes a complete meal."

Smoked Sausage Delight
LaVece Hughes

4-5 large potatoes
1 large onion, sliced
1 medium bell pepper, sliced
1 medium head cabbage

2 lb smoked sausage
season to taste—salt, pepper,
    and Cavender's seasoning
¾ to 1 c water

Slice potatoes ¼ to ½ inch thick in bottom of large roasting pan. Slice onion and Bell pepper and put on top of potatoes. Season at this time to taste. Chop cabbage and put on top of the potatoes, onions and bell pepper. Season a little more, if desired. Slice the smoked sausage into rounds about ¼ to ½ inch thick and scatter over the top of cabbage, covering completely. Pour the water over all of this. Cover with foil or lid and bake in a 350 degree oven for 1 to 1½ hours or until potatoes are done.

Note: This is just great and will feed a bunch of hungry people. It keeps well covered in the refrigerator and makes great leftovers.

You could also use chicken instead of the smoked sausage, and maybe even use cooked ground beef.

Mexican Roll-ups
Susan Hughes

1 8 oz pkg cream cheese softened
2 c shredded cheese
   (Cheddar or Mexican blend)
Flour tortillas

½ c chopped green onions
½ c chopped black olives
½ c chopped green chilies

Combine ingredients and mix. Spread mixture on tortillas. Roll and let refrigerate for 1 hour. Slice and serve with salsa.

Italian Sausage & Pepperoni Casserole
LaVece Hughes

6 links hot Italian sausage
8 oz pepperoni, diced
16 oz linguine noodles
1 medium green pepper, chopped
2 cloves garlic, minced

1 15-oz can pizza sauce
1 t oregano
1 t basil
salt and pepper to taste
8 oz shredded mozzarella cheese

Remove sausage from casing and break into small pieces, brown in skillet with pepperoni, onion, green pepper, garlic and spices; brown until tender. Boil noodles using pkg instructions, drain and combine all items. Stir to blend. Add pizza sauce and 4 oz shredded cheese, blend again. Use a greased 13x9-baking dish. Place mixture and sprinkle remaining cheese on top and add Parmesan cheese if desired. Bake for 35-40 minutes uncovered in a 350-degree oven.

Quick Skillet Supper
LaVece Hughes

1 lb ground beef, browned and
   drained
1 can beef broth
½ t salt
¼ t black pepper
1 c sour cream

2 cans mixed vegetables or
   16 oz frozen vegetables
7 oz pkg elbow macaroni
   (2 cups uncooked)
1 can French fried onions,
   divided in half

Mix drained beef with all other ingredients except sour cream and onions. (Do not cook macaroni before mixing with other ingredients.) Simmer for about 20 minutes, and then add sour cream and ½ can of the onions. Top with the other half of the onions and serve.

Italian Spaghetti . . . the quick way
Edward Hughes

2 pkg of Italian link sausage
1 large jar Prego spaghetti sauce, or your choice
1 lb spaghetti
1 can mushroom pieces
Shredded mozzarella cheese

Brown the sausage in a skillet. Skin one of the pkgs of sausage and leave the other as links before browning. Take sausage out of skillet when browned and drain on paper. Cook spaghetti in boiling water. Put spaghetti sauce, sausage, and mushrooms in another pan and heat thoroughly. Drain spaghetti. Serve topped with sauce and shredded mozzarella cheese.

"The secret is not in the sauce, it's in the meat!"

Spareribs Hawaiian
Pat Martin Dickinson

2 lb lean spareribs	½ c water
3 T flour	½ c pineapple juice
1 t salt	⅔ c wine vinegar
3 T soy sauce	1 t grated ginger root or
3 T salad oil	½ t dry ginger
⅔ c sugar	2 c pineapple and papaya chunks

Cut spareribs into 2-inch pieces. Mix flour, salt and soy sauce together and coat ribs. Allow to stand 10 minutes. Heat oil in skillet and brown ribs on all sides. Drain off excess fat and add sugar, vinegar, water, juice and ginger. Cover and simmer until meat is tender—about 45 minutes. Stir in fruit and simmer 5 minutes linger. Garnish with Sesame seeds.

"I make more coating for ribs than recipe calls for. I found this recipe in Hawaii while visiting my husband on his R & R leave in 1969."

They are not gone who live in the hearts they left behind.
— Native American Proverb

Steak and Potato Casserole
LaVece Hughes

6 medium potatoes, sliced ½ inch thick
4 cube steaks, floured
Vegetable oil

2 T flour
1 can onion soup
1 soup can of water

Cook potatoes, salted, until tender, but not done. While potatoes are boiling, flour steaks and fry in oil until browned. Pour off oil and save. Cut the steak into wide strips. Return oil to skillet and stir in flour, soup, and one can of the water that the potatoes were boiled in. Place potatoes, steak, salt and pepper in a baking dish and pour the thickened soup over them. Bake 30 minutes at 400 degrees.

Taco Soup
LaVece Hughes

1 lb ground chuck
1 large onion, chopped
3 15-oz cans Mexican style
    chili beans, with liquid
15-oz can whole kernel corn,
    with liquid
14-oz can diced tomatoes,
    with liquid
4½-oz can chopped green
    Chilies

1 envelope taco seasoning mix
1 envelope Ranch style dressing mix
1½ c water
15-oz can tomato sauce

Toppings:
corn chips, shredded lettuce, chopped tomato, sour cream, shredded cheddar cheese

Cook beef and onions in a large pot over medium-high heat until meat is browned and onions are tender, stirring until meat crumbles; drain. Stir beans and rest of ingredients into beef mixture; bring to a boil. Reduce heat, and simmer, uncovered, 15 minutes, stirring occasionally. Serve in bowls and top with desired toppings.

"I am not required to attend every argument to which I am invited ."
— Kelly Wingate

Quick Baked Tamale
LaVece Hughes

1 lb hamburger
2 T salt
⅛ t pepper
2 T chili powder

¾ c onion, chopped
16-oz can tomatoes
16-oz can whole corn, drained
1 pkg cornbread mix

Brown meat and drain. Add seasonings and onion. Add corn and tomatoes. Bring to a boil. Pour into a 9 by 13 in pan. Prepare cornbread mix according to directions and spread over mixture. Bake at 400 for 40 minutes.

Tuna Quiche
Selma Goodman Dickinson from Jane T. Goodman

½ c mayonnaise
1 c milk
½ lb cheddar cheese
bunches)
1 t Dijon mustard
1 7-oz can tuna
Pinch of salt

2 eggs
1 t cornstarch
⅓ c chopped green onions (2 small

½ t pepper
½ t Worcestershire sauce

Mix all ingredients. Pour in 9" pie shell. Bake at 350 degrees for 50 minutes.

Tuna Tempters
LaVece Hughes

1 6-7 oz can tuna
½ c cheddar cheese, shredded
½ c celery, sliced
⅓ c olives, sliced
¼ c salad dressing

2 T onion chopped
2 T pickle relish
2 hard boiled eggs, chopped
4 or more hamburger buns, split
and buttered

In a bowl, mix all the ingredients, except buns. Put mixture on buns and wrap each in foil. Bake at 350 degrees for 20 minutes. Serves six.

Tuna or Salmon Rice Au Gratin
LaVece Hughes

¼ c margarine
½ c chopped celery
2 T minced onion
2 T flour
1 t salt
dash of pepper
8 oz shredded American cheese

1 10½-oz can cream of mushroom soup
1 c milk
2 c cooked rice
12-16 oz canned salmon or tuna, drained,
    boned and flaked
buttered Ritz cracker crumbs

Melt butter in saucepan, and celery and onion, and cook until onion is transparent. Add flour and seasonings. Add milk and soup, stirring until sauce is smooth. Blend sauce with remaining ingredients and pour into buttered casserole dish. Top with buttered cracker crumbs. Bake at 350 degrees for 25-30 minutes.

Turketti
Mildred Dickinson

1¼ c spaghetti in 2-inch pieces
1½ to 2 c cut-up turkey or chicken
¼ c green pepper, chopped
½ small onion, chopped
¼ c diced pimento

1 can cream of mushroom soup
½ c broth or water
1¾ c grated sharp cheddar cheese
1 small can mushrooms, drained

Cook spaghetti, rinse, combine, saving one cup of cheese to sprinkle over top. Bake covered in casserole in 350-degree oven about 45 minutes. Serves six to nine.

"Conflict is inevitable, but combat is optional."
— Max Lucade

"Respect is love in plain clothes."
— Frankie Byne

Quiche Lorraine
Selma Goodman Dickinson from Jane S. Goodman

Pie shell
3½-oz can French Fried Onions
4 eggs
1½ c (6 oz) shredded processed American
    sharp cheddar cheese (Cracker Barrel)

½ t salt
dash cayenne pepper
2 c milk

Prepare a pie shell and cook for 7-8 minutes at 450 degrees. Reduce heat to 325 degrees. While pastry is still warm, fill with ½ cup French fried onions - reserve rest for garnish. Beat eggs slightly blend in milk and ½ cup cheese, salt and pepper. Pour over onions in shell. Sprinkle 1 cup cheese over this. Bake at 325 for 45 minutes. Sprinkle onions over top. Bake 5-10 minutes more until knife inserted in center comes out clean. Let stand 10 minutes before serving to come to room temperature.

Reuben Sandwiches for Four
LaVece Hughes

8 slices of pumpernickel bread
1 lb of thinly sliced corned
    beef (from a deli)
½ c of well-drained sauerkraut**

3 T of thousand island dressing
4 slices of Swiss Cheese
2 T of margarine or butter

Top 4 slices of bread with corned beef, then sauerkraut, salad dressing, and cheese.
Top with other bread slices. Spread margarine on outsides of each sandwich.
Grill on hot griddle, skillet, or under broiler until bread is browned and cheese melts.

** To make sure sauerkraut is totally drained, place it in 2 or 3 layers of paper towels and squeeze out the excess fluid.

Privilege is invisible to those who have it.

Rice Meatballs
LaVece Hughes

1 c uncooked Minute Rice
1 lb ground beef
1 egg, slightly beaten
2 t chopped onion

2 t salt
3 cups tomato juice
1 t salt
dash pepper

Mix rice with beef, egg, onions salt and pepper and ½ cup of the tomato juice. Shape into balls and put in a skillet. Add sugar to remaining juice and pour over meatballs. Bring to a boil and reduce heat, cover and simmer about 15 minutes.

Turkey Brunch
LaVece Hughes

1 c turkey, cooked and diced
1 c cheddar cheese
1 egg, beaten well
3 English muffins, split

6 T mayonnaise
dash Tabasco sauce
pinch of salt

Mix turkey, cheese, egg, mayonnaise, Tabasco sauce, and salt together. Place mixture on muffins and bake in a 375-degree oven for 8 –10 minutes or until lightly browned and puffy.

Woodchuck Stew . . . strange name, but good!
LaVece Hughes

Medium-thick sauce in large pan:
3 c milk
1 stick butter
½ c cornstarch

1 t curry powder (or to taste)
salt and pepper to taste

Add to this sauce:
2 c cut up chicken or turkey
2 c small shrimp

6 hard-boiled eggs, chopped
1 small jar chopped pimento

Serve over plain white rice, wild rice or a mixture. Sprinkle Chinese or rice noodles over the woodchuck. Serve over rice. Makes eight servings.

Pies

Best Ever Apple Dumplings
Willette Saunders

Pie Crust:
1 c flour
2 T shortening, heaping
3 T water

(Or use prepared crust)

Mix and roll out for
dumplings.

Vanilla Sauce:
1 c sugar
1 T flour
2 c water

Stir and bring to a boil. Add:
1 t vanilla
1 T butter

Use 3 medium apples, slice thin and put in bowl, sprinkle with sugar, 1 T
flour and a little nutmeg. Place on pastry squares. Add 4 cinnamon red
hots to each. Pinch together. Put in an 8 x 8 pan and bake at 400
degrees. As soon as they are in the oven make sauce. By the time it
boils, dumplings should be starting to brown on top. Pour thin sauce over
dumplings and continue baking until done. Sauce will have cooked up
quite a bit. Serve with ice cream or whipped cream.

Willette said that this was the best thing she'd ever eaten.

Baked Apple Dumplings
LaVece Hughes

Pastry sheets (available in
    freezer section of grocery)
Granny Smith apples

cinnamon sticks for each apple
1 jar apricot preserves
brown sugar

Thaw and unfold pastry sheets. Core and peel Granny Smith apples and
each in center of a sheet of puff pastry, trimming to make a circle. Insert
a cinnamon stick in hollow; spoon in 1 teaspoon apricot preserves, 1
tablespoon brown sugar. Lightly brush exposed pastry with water.
Repeat with remaining apples. Fold up pastry, smoothing over apple,
pressing folds to seal and gathering corners at top. Trim excess. Brush
each dumpling with milk and sprinkle with granulated sugar. Bake in a
350-degree oven for 30-35 minutes until pastry is golden brown.

Berry Apple Pie
LaVece Hughes

1 c sugar
1 t quick cooking tapioca
½ t cinnamon
2 prepared crusts, uncooked

2 c blackberries or blueberries
2 c sliced, peeled apples
2 T butter, cut up

Mix and let sit for 15 minutes. Pour into 9½-inch pie pan lined with piecrust. Cover with second crust. Sprinkle with sugar. Cook for 25 minutes in a 375-degree oven.

Blackberry Cobbler
LaVece Hughes from Kate Ganter

Crust:
3 cups flour
12 T shortening
6 T water

Cobbler:
2 qt blackberries
3 c sugar
3 T flour
½ c water
4 T butter

Put blackberries in large pan. Dump the 3 T flour, 3 cups sugar, and ½ cup water on top of berries, gently stirring to mix in flour. While preparing crust, heat berries just to a boil on medium high heat.

In mixing bowl, cut shortening into flour and add water. Mix dough thoroughly. Flour wax paper and roll dough out between two pieces into a rectangle about 12 x 20 inches. Use extra flour to prevent crust from sticking to wax paper. Remove wax paper from one side of crust and turn over into the bottom corner of a 13 x 9 inch Pyrex dish, leaving the rest of the crust hanging over the edge of the other side.
After berries have just come to a boil, pour into dish and dot with about 4 T butter. Flip the rest of the crust over the top of the berries and tuck into the opposite side. Sprinkle sugar over the top. Bake for 35 minutes at 375 degrees.

This is the" old time" way of making blackberry cobbler passed down from my Grandmother Lelia Dickinson. It makes lots of juice.

Blackberry Cobbler
Willette Saunders

2 c fresh blackberries (or can)
1 c flour
½ c sugar
1 t baking powder

1 stick butter, melted
½ c milk
½ t vanilla
½ c hot water
½ c sugar

Preheat oven to 350 degrees. Place blackberries in a 9 x 9 pan. Combine butter, flour, ½ c sugar, baking powder, milk and vanilla. Pour over fruit. Combine water and ½ c sugar. Pour over flour mixture. Bake for 55 minutes or till done.

Blackberry Camp Meeting Pie
Mamaw Mattox from Marsha Williams

1 stick butter
1 c flour
1 c sugar

1 t baking powder
1 qt blackberries or other fruit

Melt butter in a 13 x 9 inch dish in the oven. Mix flour, sugar and baking powder in a bowl. Pour batter over the melted butter. Do not stir. Heat fruit and pour on top of butter/batter mixture. Do not stir. Bake at 350 degrees for 30 minutes or until golden brown on top.

"Mamaw was the cook at a church camp in the sixties and this pie was a favorite of all those who attended."

Quick Cherry Crisp
LaVece Dickinson

1 can cherry pie filling
¼ c margarine

Jiffy Cake Mix (or 1 c cake mix)
½ c chopped nuts (optional)

Butter a 9-inch square Pyrex dish. Pour 1 can cherry pie filling into dish. Mix margarine with cake mix. Sprinkle cake mixture over filling. Bake at 350 degrees for 45-50 minutes.

Blueberry Roll
LaVece Hughes

1 c flour
½ c chopped pecans
1 stick butter
¼ c brown sugar

1 can blueberry pie filling
8 oz cream cheese softened
¾ c sugar
1 c cool whip, thawed

Cream butter and sugar until fluffy. Add flour and pecans and mix well. Spray a 9 x 13 pan with vegetable oil. Press the pecan mixture in bottom of pan and slightly up the sides. Bake at 325 degrees for 15 – 20 minutes until lightly browned. Cool. Beat cream cheese until fluffy. Gradually beat in sugar. Fold in cool whip. Spread mixture over crust. Spread blueberry pie filling over cream cheese mixture. Cover and chill until firm.

Blueberry Surprise
LaVece Hughes

1 stick margarine, melted
1 c flour

¼ c brown sugar
1 c nuts, chopped

Mix all together and press into a 9 x 12 inch pan. Bake for 15 minutes at 350 degrees. Cool completely. Then mix:

1 c sugar
8 oz Cool Whip

8 oz cream cheese
1 t vanilla

Spread onto cooled crust and top with a can of blueberry pie filling (cherry or other flavors can be used as well.) Refrigerate at least one hour before serving.

"How much butter is that?"
1 stick of butter = 7½ tablespoons = almost a half cup (8 oz)

Buttermilk Pie
Maggie Jones

2 c sugar
5 T flour
½ c melted butter
3 eggs

1 t vanilla
1 c buttermilk
1 unbaked pie shell

Mix well and pour into unbaked pie shell. Cook at 350 degrees for 45 minutes.

Cherry Pie . . . 90 seconds preparation
LaVece Hughes

15 oz prepared pkg of refrigerated pie crusts
1 can cherry pie filling

Place one crust in bottom of a 9-inch pie pan. Pour in a can of pie filling. Cut second crust into strips. Alternate strips vertically and horizontally over the pie. Crimp edges with a fork. Sprinkle sugar on top and cook for 30 minutes at 350 degrees until browned.

Butterscotch Pie
LaVece Hughes

½ c brown sugar
½ c white sugar
4 T flour
1 stick butter

1 c milk
3 eggs, separated
pinch salt
1 baked pie shell

Mix sugar, flour and salt, add milk slowly while mixing, and then butter. Cook and stir until it begins to get thick. Add some of hot mix to egg yolks and return to heat. Cook till very thick. Put in baked pie shell and top with meringue.

Meringue:
Beat 3 egg whites in glass mixing bowl until soft peaks form. Add 1 t vanilla and
6 T of sugar gradually, beating until stiff peaks form. Spread over pie, sealing to edge, and bake in a 325 degree oven for 15 minutes or until lightly brown.

Chess Pie
LaVece Dickinson

½ c margarine
2 c sugar
1 T corn meal
1 can of Pet milk

½ c egg yolks (6)
1 T flour
1 T vanilla
1 unbaked pie crust

Combine and pour into an unbaked pie shell. Bake for 15 minutes at 375 degrees, and then turn down the oven to 325 degrees for 30 minutes until lightly browned.

Chocolate Chess Pie
Becky Kays

1¼ c sugar
¼ c margarine
10 T evaporated milk
¼ c cocoa

2 eggs
1½ t vanilla
1 unbaked pie crust

Mix sugar, cocoa and melted margarine in medium bowl. Add eggs; beat well. Blend in milk and vanilla. Bake in pie shell at 350 degrees until tester comes out clear, 35–40 minutes.

Chocolate Pie . . . yummy and never fails
Christian Church Homes of Kentucky Cookbook

3 egg yolks, beaten
1½ c sugar
¼ c flour
2 t butter
2 heaping T cocoa

1 t vanilla
1¾ c evaporated milk
1 baked 9 inch pie shell
3 egg whites
6 T sugar
1 t vanilla

Place egg yolks, and sifted 1½ cup sugar and flour into a saucepan. Stir in butter, cocoa, vanilla and evaporated milk. Cook over medium heat until thickened, stirring constantly. Pour into pie shell. Beat egg whites in glass mixing bowl until soft peaks form. Add vanilla and 6 T of sugar gradually, beating until stiff peaks form. Spread over pie, sealing to edge and bake in a 325 degree oven for 15 minutes or until lightly brown.

Always a great chocolate pie.— lgh

Ice Cream Sandwich Dessert
LaVece Hughes

19 ice cream sandwiches
12 oz cool whip, thawed

12 oz hot fudge topping
1 c salted peanuts

Cut one ice cream sandwich in half. Place one whole and one half sandwich along a short side of and un-greased 13 x 9 pan. Arrange eight sandwiches in opposite direction in the pan. Spread with half of the whipped topping. Spoon ½ of the fudge topping by teaspoonfuls onto whipped topping. Sprinkle with ½ cup peanuts. Repeat layers with remaining ice cream sandwiches, whipped topping and peanuts (pan will be full). Cover and freeze for up to 2 months. Remove from the freezer 20 minutes before serving. Cut into squares. Serves 12-15.

"My family loves this dessert and it can be made and brought out months later. You can't tell it is made from ice cream sandwiches.— lgh

Coconut Cream Pie
Inez Dickinson from Grandma Schneider

10 inch pie:
1½ c sugar
2 ½ T melted butter
3 eggs
1½ c sweet milk
2 c fresh grated coconut (or 1
    pkg frozen grated)
1 t vanilla
Dash salt

9 inch pie:
1 c sugar
2 T butter
2 eggs
1 c milk
1½ c coconut
1 t vanilla
Dash salt

Cream butter and sugar together. Then add eggs, one at a time while mixing. About 1 T of milk will mike it cream better. Mix in milk slowly and add vanilla and coconut. Pour into uncooked pie shell. Bake at 400 degrees for 10 minutes; then at 375 for 20 to 25 minutes until custard part of pie is set and top is browned. If pie is browning too fast, turn oven down to 350 degrees to finish baking.

Cranberry Walnut Pie
The Jessamine Elves

1 shortbread pie crust
¾ c chopped walnuts
2 cans apple pie filling
¼ t nutmeg

6-oz bag sweetened dried cranberries
⅓ c flour
¼ c brown sugar, packed
3 T butter, melted

Heat oven to 375 degrees. Mix apple pie filling, cranberries and nutmeg. Spoon into crust. Combine flour and sugar; cut in butter until crumbly. Stir in walnuts; sprinkle over filing. Bake 35-45 minutes or until topping is golden

"First Saturday in May" Pie
Susan Brown

¾ c sugar
¾ c flour
2 eggs, lightly beaten
½ c butter, melted
1½ c chocolate chips

1 t vanilla
1 T bourbon
½ c chopped pecans
1 9-inch pie crust

Bake crust for 10 minutes at 350 degrees. Remove and reduce oven temperature to 325 degrees. Mix sugar and flour together. Add eggs and butter. Stir in remaining ingredients and mix well. Pour filling into the partially baked pie shell. Bake at 325 degrees for 50-60 minutes until lightly browned.

This pie is as good as, if not better, than Kern's Derby Pie. — lgh

*"40% of the world's resources are owned by 6% of the world's population
And those 6% reside in Canada and the USA." — Mike Richey*

Japanese Pie
Janice Underwood

1 stick margarine, melted
¾ c raisins
¾ c coconut
¾ c chopped pecans
2 beaten eggs

1 c white sugar
4 t flour
1 T vinegar
1 unbaked deep pie shell

Mix all ingredients well and pour into an unbaked pie shell. Bake at 350 degrees for 40 minutes. Freezes well.

This is similar to Derby Pie, but with raisins and coconut. — lgh

Sour Cream Lemon Pie
Linda Gallagher of Linda's Sandwich Shop

1 9-inch baked pie crust
¾ c sugar
3 T cornstarch
1 c milk
3 eggs, separated
juice of 2 lemons

Zest of a lemon
3 T butter
1 c sour cream
3 T sugar
⅜ t cream of tartar
1 t vanilla

Combine ¾ cup of sugar, cornstarch, milk, and egg yolks in saucepan and cook over medium heat until very thick. Add lemon juice and some zest. Add butter and sour cream. Pour into the baked piecrust and top with meringue.

Meringue:
Beat egg white until frothy. Add 3 T sugar and cream of tartar. Beat until soft peaks form. Pour on top of hot pie filling and spread evenly to edges of crust. Bake at 350 degrees oven until meringue begins to brown; about 20 minutes.

"When you speak, your words echo down the hall,
But when you write, your words echo down the ages."
— Jerry Oughton,
Music From a Place Called Half Moon

Lemonade Pie
LaVece Hughes

6-oz can frozen lemonade, thawed
1 can Eagle Brand Milk
12-oz container cool whip

29-oz can crushed pineapple, drained
3 oz Philadelphia cream cheese, softened
Graham cracker pie shell

Mix ingredients together and pour into a graham cracker crust. Chill overnight.

Lemon Meringue Pie
Lelia Handy with help from Cousin Betty Crocker

4 eggs
½ c sugar
3 T flour
3 T cornstarch
1½ c water

2 T margarine
1½ t grated lemon peel
⅓ c lemon juice
1 cooked pie shell

Mix sugar, flour, cornstarch and dash of salt. Gradually stir in water over medium heat until thickened and bubbly. Reduce heat and cook 2 minutes more. Remove from heat; slightly beat egg yolks. Gradually stir in 1 cup of hot filling into yolks. Pour into rest of mixture. Bring to gentle boil. Cook and stir 2 minutes more. Remove from heat and stir in margarine and lemon zest peel. Stir in lemon juice and pour into a cooked pie shell. Top with meringue and bake for 15 minutes at 350 degrees.

Meringue

4 egg whites
1 t vanilla

½ t cream of tartar
8 T sugar

Beat egg whites about 1 minute until foamy. Add rest of ingredients and beat until stiff peaks.

Some people make the world special just by being in it.
— Tricia O'Kelly

Lemon Chess Pie
Kate Ganter

4 eggs
2 c sugar
1 T grated lemon rind
¼ c lemon juice
¼ c butter, melted

1 T cornmeal
1 T flour
¼ c milk
pinch salt
1 uncooked pie shell

Beat eggs; gradually add sugar. Stir in remaining ingredients. Pour into unbaked pie shell. Bake 350 degrees for 45 – 50 minutes or until brown. Do not over bake.

Lemon Delight Dessert
LaVece Hughes

1 stick butter
1 c self-rising flour
8 oz cream cheese
1 c powdered sugar

2 c Cool Whip
2 boxes lemon instant pudding
3 c milk

Melt butter; combine with flour and press into an 13 x 9 Pyrex pan and bake in a 400-degree oven until golden brown about 15 minutes. Mix cream cheese, powdered sugar and one cup of Cool Whip. Spread onto cooled crust. Mix pudding and milk and spread over cream cheese mixture. Spread remaining Cool Whip over top and keep refrigerated

Creamy Lemon Pies
LaVece Hughes

1¾ c cold milk
1 6-oz can frozen lemonade
    concentrate, thawed

2 4-oz boxes vanilla instant pudding
1 8-oz cool whip, thawed
2 6-oz graham cracker crusts

Pour milk in large bowl, adding pudding mix, and beat 30 seconds. Add lemonade and beat 30 seconds more. Mix in cool whip and pour into crusts. Refrigerate 4 hours.

Lemon Pie with Meringue Crust. . . unique
Ann Vanzant

Crust:
3 jumbo egg whites at room
    temperature
¼ t cream of tartar
1 c sugar

Add sugar and cream of tartar gradually to egg whites and beat until meringue forms stiff peaks. Spread into 2 large buttered pie plates. Bake at 300 degrees for 1 hour. Cool on rack.

Filling:
2 small pkgs cook-and-serve
    Lemon pie filling
16 oz cool whip, thawed

Cook pudding according to directions on boxes. Cool. Stir in 8 oz of cool whip. Spread filling evenly in pie shells then spread rest of cool whip on top of pies.

Shaker Lemon Pie
Shakertown at Pleasant Hill, Kentucky

2 large lemons
2 c sugar

4 eggs, well beaten
2 9-inch unbaked pie shell

Slice unpeeled lemons paper-thin. Remove seeds, add sugar and mix well. Let stand 2 hours or longer, stirring occasionally. Thoroughly blend eggs into the lemon mixture. Turn into an unbaked pie shell, arranging lemon slices evenly. Slice the remaining pie shell to make a vented top. Bake at 450 degrees for 15 minutes; reduce the heat to 375 degrees and cook for 20 minutes until "a silver knife inserted near the edge comes out clean."

Martha Stewart recently enjoyed this recipe on a visit to Shakertown near Harrodsburg, Kentucky, and took two pies home with her.

"Even if you are in the right track, you'll
get run over if you just sit there."
— Will Rogers

Key Lime Pie
LaVece Hughes

1 pie shell, baked and cooled

Filling:
1 can sweetened condensed milk
1 T grated key lime rind
½ c lime juice
¼ t salt
2 slightly beaten egg yolks

Meringue:
3 egg whites
3 T sugar
Beat until foamy then gradually
mix in sugar and beat until stiff
peaks form.

Stir all filling ingredients until thickened (a result of a reaction to the milk
and lime juice). (Optional: 2-3 drops green cake coloring) Pour into crust,
and cover with meringue. Bake for 10-15 minutes at 350 degrees until
lightly browned.

Strawberry Tarts . . . quick and very good
LaVece Hughes

6 Graham Cracker tart shells
1 c strawberry gel (found in
    produce department)
1½ c sliced strawberries

4 oz cream cheese, softened
½ c sugar
1 T sour cream
1 t vanilla

Slice strawberries and mix with gel. Combine cream cheese, sugar, sour
cream, and vanilla and place a heaping tablespoon is each shell. Spoon
strawberries and gel on top in each tart.

Lucky-To-Have-Any-Left Pie
Betty Mulberry

First layer:
2 c flour
2 stick butter
1 c pecans

Mix and press into 13 x 9 in
Pyrex pan. Bake for 20 minutes
in a 325-degree oven. Cool.

Second layer:
1 8-oz cream cheese
1 c powdered sugar
1 9-oz cool whip

Mix with mixer and spread over
crust.

Third layer:
2 small pkgs butter-pecan
    Instant pudding mix
3½ c milk

Mix well and pour over 2nd layer

Fourth layer:
9 oz cool whip
¾ c chopped pecans

Put on top of 3rd layer and
sprinkle with chopped pecans

Ozark Pie
Nonnie Evans . . . Judged best dessert, What's Cooking in the Bluegrass, *1982*

¾ c sugar
¾ c flour
1 egg
1¼ t baking powder

⅛ t salt
1 c apples, cut up
1 c pecans, chopped
1 t vanilla

Beat egg. Add sugar. Add sifted flour, salt, baking powder. Add nuts, apples, and vanilla. Spread and bake in a buttered 8-inch pie pan at 350 degrees for 35 minutes. Serve with whipped cream or ice cream.

Peach Delight
LaVece Hughes

32 oz peaches, with juice
½ c pecans

Butter Pecan Cake mix
6 oz melted butter

Pour peaches into 9 x 11 Pyrex pan. Sprinkle dry cake mix on top. Sprinkle pecans over the cake mix and pour melted butter on top. Bake for 1 hour at 350.

Peach Crisp
LaVece Hughes

Pie Filling:
1 29-oz can sliced peaches
2 T cornstarch
¼ t cinnamon
½ c lemon juice
½ c chopped pecans

1 c packed brown sugar
1 T honey
¼ t nutmeg
½ c raisins

Topping:
1 c flour
½ c sugar

½ c melted butter
optional: vanilla ice cream

Pie Filling:
Drain peaches, reserving syrup in saucepan. Set peaches aside. Stir brown sugar, cornstarch, honey, cinnamon, nutmeg and syrup until smooth. Bring to boil and stir for 2 minutes until thick. Add lemon juice, pecans, and peaches. Pour into greased 2 qt dish.

Topping:
Combine flour, sugar and butter. Sprinkle over peach mixture. Bake 350 degrees for 35 minutes. Serve with ice cream if desired.

To prevent a bottom piecrust from becoming soggy, grease pie pans with margarine. The crust will be soft and flaky. — Betty Hammond

Need a recipe? Try www.foodtv.com

Peanut Butter Chiffon Pie
Liz Woodward

1 envelope unflavored gelatin
½ c boiling water
8 oz cream cheese
1 c powdered sugar

½ c favorite peanut butter
8 oz cool whip
1 9-in graham cracker crust
¼ c finely chopped peanuts, optional

Dissolve gelatin in boiling water. Cool to lukewarm. Whip cheese until soft and fluffy. Beat in sugar and peanut butter. Slowly add gelatin mixture, blending thoroughly. Fold cool whip into mixture. Chill until firm, 1 - 2 hours. Optional: Drizzle with Hershey's chocolate syrup before serving.

Pineapple Coconut Pie
LaVece Hughes

1½ cups sugar
1 c crushed pineapple
   (do not drain)
3 lightly beaten eggs

3 T flour
1 c flaked coconut
¾ stick margarine
1 unbaked pie shell

Preheat oven to 350 degrees. Stir together sugar, pineapple, eggs, flour and coconut in a bowl. Melt butter and add to other ingredients. Pour filling into pie shell. Bake 1 hour or until filling is set and brown

Two Pecans Pies
Emmy Lou Dickinson, from My Cousin's Kitchen

2 unbaked pie shell
½ c margarine, melted
5 eggs, well beaten
1 c coconut

2 c sugar
1½ c dark corn syrup
1 T lemon juice
¾ c pecans

Mix all ingredients and place in 2 pie shells. Bake at 425 degrees for 10 min, reduce heat to 300 degrees and bake for 50 min. Will freeze.

Pineapple Meringue . . . a family favorite

LaVece Dickinson

8 egg whites	2 c sugar
½ t salt	1 large can of crushed pineapple,
2 t vanilla	partially drained
1 T vinegar	8 oz cool whip

Preheat oven to 450 degrees. Beat egg whites, salt, vanilla and vinegar on high speed until soft peaks appear. Gradually add sugar, small amount at a time until stiff peaks appear. Divide into two 9-inch cake pans lined with brown paper bags cut to fit. Grease only on side next to pan. Turn oven down to 300 degrees and bake for one hour. Cool on wire racks. Can store for several days before using.

Run a knife around edge of pan to remove meringue, and peel off paper. Place on serving dish with a lip. Partially drain the pineapple and spread half on top of first layer. Top with ⅓ of the cool whip. Add second layer and top with remaining pineapple and cream.
(Meringues will keep in pans for days.)

Granddaughter Becky's Variation:
Add red food coloring to the meringue and use fresh strawberries, cut and sugared, instead of crushed pineapple.

"I sometimes use 1 cup of fresh strawberries, cut and sugared, with the can of crushed pineapple, and strawberry-flavored Cool Whip instead of plain Cool Whip. Yumm"— lgh

"No one can make you feel inferior without your consent."
—Eleanor Roosevelt

147

The Dickinson Pumpkin Pie

Lelia Anderson Trabue

1 c cooked pumpkin
1 egg
1 T cream or milk
1 c sugar
¼ t cinnamon

½ to 1 t allspice
¼ t nutmeg
¼ ginger
1 T melted butter
1 unbaked pie shell

Beat egg, add sugar, spices, cream, pumpkin and melted butter. Blend. Pour into unbaked crust; bake 10 minutes at 450 degrees, then 30 minutes at 350 degrees. Serve with whipped cream.

This recipe has been handed down in my family for seven generations. It is THE Dickinson Pumpkin Pie recipe that my Aunt 'Nez Dickinson sent to The Courier Journal's *Cissy Greg, in contradiction to an editorial that stated "the best place for pumpkins was to leave them in the field." Aunt 'Nez wrote "I didn't like pumpkin pie either, until I married and moved to Kentucky from Louisiana." "Then," she wrote, "I ate a piece of pumpkin pie made by my husband's mother, Mrs. B.G. Dickinson, from a recipe handed down from her grandmother [Lelia Anderson Trabue] and I changed my mind!"*

Aunt 'Nez recommended that the pie was never to be eaten stone cold, but I have known Dickinsons to eat it in any form, at any time, even for breakfast. My mother would reduce the sugar to ¾ c and triple this recipe and put it into two pies." — lgh

Pumpkin Pecan Pie

Nancy Reagan, former First Lady

4 slightly beaten eggs
2 c canned or mashed
    cooked pumpkin
1 c sugar
½ c dark corn syrup

1 t vanilla
½ t cinnamon
¼ t salt
1 unbaked 9 inch pie shell
1 c chopped pecans

Combine ingredients except pecans. Pour into pie shell and top with pecans. Bake at 350 degrees for 40 minutes or until set.

Pie Crust

Mary Lynn Dickinson

2 c flour
11 T shortening

5-6 T ice water
1 t salt

Sift flour into a mixing bowl. Add shortening and cut with pastry blender or 2 forks. Mix ice water and salt together and add to flour mixture by tossing with fingertips. Roll out on wax paper into a 10-inch circle and place in pie dish. Turn under edges and pinch with fingers or a fork. Cook for 12–15 minutes in a 450-degree oven.

Avondel Hart recommends that you add ½ teaspoon baking powder for each cup of flour. The baking powder makes for a much lighter pie shell. — lgh

Rhubarb Pie

Leslie Webb from Louise White

2 c rhubarb, cut in ½ inch pieces
1 c sugar
3 T flour

2 T butter or margarine
2 unbaked pie shells

Mix rhubarb, sugar and flour together and place in unbaked pie shell. Cut butter up over the mixture. Add top crust. Seal and puncture this crust with a fork. Sprinkle with sugar and bake for 45 minutes in a 350 degree oven.

"My Grandmother, Louise White ran a grocery store in Waterford, Kentucky. She would write recipes from her customers on small brown bags from the store. This was one of those recipes."

"Before you say what you think ... think what you are going to say."
—Beth Brock

The Best Apple Stuff, Ever
LaVece Hughes

4 apples, peeled and sliced thin
1½ cups water (pour over
    apples)
½ c sugar (sprinkle on top)

1 dry white or yellow cake mix
1½ sticks melted margarine
cinnamon (sift on top)
1 c chopped pecans or almonds

Spray a 9 x 13 baking dish with Pam and layer ingredients in the order listed. Bake at 375 degrees for 45 minutes. Serve warm or cold.

4-Layer Chocolate Dessert . . . a family favorite
LaVece Hughes

First layer
1½ c flour
1¼ stick butter (10 T)

½ c chopped pecans

Mix and pat into 9 x 13 inch Pyrex pan. Cook for 20 minutes in a 375 degrees oven. Cool

Second Layer
8 oz Cream Cheese
1 c powdered sugar

½ large carton Kool Whip
optional: (¼ c peanut butter)

Mix and pour over cooled crust.

Third Layer
2 small boxes instant chocolate pudding *   3 cups milk

Spread pudding over 2nd layer

Fourth Layer
Spread remaining Kool Whip and sprinkle with chopped pecans.

* our family prefers chocolate, but other flavors may be substituted.

Peanut Butter Chocolate Dessert
Ed Hughes

25 Oreo cookies, divided
2 T margarine, melted
8 oz cream cheese, softened
½ c peanut butter

1½ cups powdered sugar, divided
16 oz Kool Whip, thawed and divided
15 miniature peanut butter cups, chopped
1 c cold milk
1 small instant chocolate pudding mix

Crush Oreos and toss with the butter. Press into the bottom of an ungreased 9-inch square dish. Save about ¼ of the crushed Oreos for topping. In a mixing bowl, beat the cream cheese, peanut butter and 1 cup of the powdered sugar until smooth. Fold in half of the Kool Whip. Spread over crust carefully. Sprinkle with peanut butter cups.

Beat the milk; pudding mix and remaining powdered sugar on low speed for 2 minutes. Fold in remaining whipped topping. Spread over peanut butter cups. Sprinkle with remaining Oreo crumbs. Cover and chill for at least 3 hours. Yield: 12-16 servings

Ozark Pudding
LaVece Hughes

1 egg
2 heaping T flour
⅛ t salt
½ chopped nuts

¾ cup sugar
¼ t baking powder
½ c chopped apples
1 t vanilla

Beat egg, and sugar until light and fluffy. Sift together flour, baking powder, salt and mix with egg mixture. Fold in apples and nuts. Add vanilla. Bake 30 minutes at 325 in a buttered Pyrex dish. Serve with hard sauce.

Millionaire Pie
LaVece Hughes

I can Eagle Brand condensed
    milk (can use fat free)
9 oz cool whip
4 T lemon juice

1 lrg can crushed pineapple,
    drained, well
½ c chopped pecans
2 graham cracker crusts

Combine condensed milk and lemon juice; mix well. Fold in cool whip; stir in well-drained pineapple and pecans. Spread into 2 prepared crusts and chill.

Cakes

Apple Pie Cake
LaVece Hughes

⅔ c self rising flour
1¾ c sugar
1 t cloves
1 t nutmeg
1 heaping t cinnamon

1 t vanilla
¾ c oil
3 eggs
1 can apple pie filling
1 c pecans, chopped

Mix the dry ingredients together; add all other ingredients. Mix very well. Pour into greased and floured tube pan. Bake for 1 to 1¼ hour at 350 degrees. Cool in pan for 10 minutes before taking out.

Glaze for Cake
½-¾ box powdered sugar
½ stick margarine
½ t cinnamon

¼ t vanilla
1 T milk

Mix this to soft spreading consistency, and smooth over top of the cake.

Blackberry Cake
LaVece Hughes

2 c sugar
1 c shortening
1-2 c blackberries canned or
    fresh with ¼ c water
1 c buttermilk
1 T soda

3 eggs
3 c flour
dash of salt
1 t of cloves, nutmeg, cinnamon,
    and allspice
½ c chopped nuts

Mix all ingredients well and bake in a large sheet cake pan at 350 degrees for 35 – 40 minutes or until toothpick in center is clean. Frost with Cream Cheese Recipe below or a Caramel Icing.

Cream Cheese Icing
8-oz pkg cream cheese
1 box powdered cheese

½ c margarine
1 t vanilla

Mix all ingredients, beat well and spread on cake.

Black Forest Cake
LaVece Hughes

1 German chocolate or devil's
    food cake mix
Eggs and shortening as called
    for on the box
⅓ c plus 4 T rum

1 c mini chocolate chips
1 can cherry pie filling
16 oz cool whip
shaved chocolate and cocktail
    cherries for garnish

Prepare cake according to directions on box except substitute ⅓ cup rum for ⅓ cup of the water. When mix is prepared, stir in mini morsels. Bake in two 9-inch pans. Stir 4T rum into cherry pie filling. Allow cake to cool. Place first layer on a platter, spread ½ pie filling and ½ cool whip. Add next layer and repeat pie filling and cool whip

Boston Cream Pie
LaVece Hughes

Yellow cake mix

Filling:
2 small pkgs instant vanilla
    pudding
2 cups cool whip

Frosting:
½ c sour cream
2 T margarine, softened
2 cups powdered sugar
1 cups chocolate chips
1 t vanilla

Prepare cake according to directions. And bake in two 9–10 inch greased pans lined with wax paper. Cool in pans 10 minutes.

For filling, combine pudding and milk. Whisk until smooth and slightly thickened. Whisk in cool whip and spread in center of cake. Add second layer. For frosting, whisk sour cream and margarine until well blended. Whisk in powdered sugar and mix until blended. Melt chocolate chips in microwave and stir into sugar mixture. Stir in vanilla and enough milk to reach desired spreading consistency. Spread over pudding layer. Refrigerate and keep stored in refrigerator.

"Whoever is happy will make others happy, too!" — *Ann Frank*

Cherries Jubilee
LaVece Hughes

2 sticks butter
2 c flour
1 c pecans, chopped fine

8 oz cream cheese
1 lb confectioners sugar
4 cups cool whip
1 can cherry pie filling

Mix first 3 ingredients. Pat into 9 x 13 in pan. Bake at 400 degrees for 20 minutes. Mix cheese and sugar, fold cool whip into cheese mixture. Spread over cooled crust. Cool in refrigerator. Add 1 can cherry pie filling on top. *"It's delicious."*

Bread Pudding
Sherry Dickinson

12 slices of day old bread
1 qt milk
6 eggs

2 c sugar
1 T vanilla
1 T melted butter

Break bread in small pieces and put in large bowl. Add milk and allow soaking for 5 minutes. Beat eggs with sugar and vanilla and add to bread mixture. Pour melted butter into a 2 qt baking dish and then add bread mixture. Bake at 350 degrees for 1 hour. Serve warm with sauce.

Bourbon Sauce:
1 stick butter
1 c sugar
1 egg

¼ c water
½ c bourbon

Melt butter, add sugar and water and cook over medium heat for 5 minutes, stirring occasionally. In separate bowl beat egg. Remove butter mixture from heat; gradually add this mixture to egg whisking constantly. Add bourbon. Serve warm over bread pudding.

When you don't have time to make icing from scratch, blend a half can of chocolate frosting with 3 ounces of softened cream cheese in a mixing bowl. The creamy result is not as sweet or as thick as the canned icing, but very good.

Cinnamon Sauce . . . for bread pudding & dumplings
LaVece Hughes

⅓ c sugar
2 t cornstarch
dash salt

¼ t cinnamon
⅔ c water

Mix all ingredients over medium heat. Bring to boil, stirring frequently.
Serve warm over bread pudding, or dumplings. Add raisins if you like.
Makes ⅔ cup.

*I usually double this for the family. Pepperidge Farm makes Frozen Apple
Dumplings that make a good and quick dessert with this sauce.*

Chocolate-Amaretto Cheesecake . . . fantastic & easy
Barb Lawler

10 chocolate wafers, finely crushed
1 ½ cups light cream cheese
1 c sugar
1 c 1% low-fat cottage cheese
¼ c plus 2 T cocoa

¼ c flour
¼ c amaretto
1 t vanilla extract
¼ t salt
1 egg
2 T chocolate chips

Sprinkle chocolate wafer crumbs in bottom of a 9-inch spring form pan.
Set aside. Blend cream cheese, and next 7 ingredients, in a food
processor until smooth. Add egg and process until blended. Fold in
chocolate chips. Slowly pour mixture over crumbs in pan. Bake at 300
degrees for 65-70 minutes or until cheesecake is set. Let cool in pan on
wire rack. Cover and chill at least 8 hours. Remove sides from pan and
transfer to a serving platter.

Add topping made from 1 cup melted chocolate chips and ½ cup sour
cream.

*Old time cooks would add 2 T of vinegar to a cup of milk to make
buttermilk. — lgh*

Chocolate Cherry Upside-Down Cake
LaVece Hughes

1 box Chocolate cake mix
21-oz can cherry pie filling

Spread the cherry pie filling evenly over the bottom of a greased 13x9 baking pan. Mix the cake mix according to the directions on the box. Pour batter evenly over cherry pie filling. Bake in 350 degree oven for 30-35 minutes or till cake tests done. Cool 10 minutes in pan; invert and cool. Serve with cool whip.

Chocolate Cheese Cake
Lelia Ganter Handy

Crust:
1½ c crushed Oreo cookies
¼ margarine (melted)

Gouache Topping:
2 c whipping cream
8 oz chocolate chips

Filling:
3 8-oz cream cheese, softened
1¼ c sugar
6 eggs
1 pt sour cream
⅓ c flour
2 t vanilla
8 oz chocolate chips, melted

Crust:
Preheat oven to 350 degrees. Generously grease a 9 x 13 spring form pan with butter. Mix crust ingredients in bowl until well blended. Press mixture into bottom and sides of pan. Cook for 10 minutes

Filling:
With electric mixer on low speed or with a wooden spoon, beat cream cheese in a large bowl until soft. Gradually beat in sugar until light and fluffy. Beat in eggs, one at a time until well blended. Stir in sour cream, flour vanilla until smooth. Cool in refrigerator.

Gouache Topping:
The next day, warm cream to just beginning to boil, and take off the stove. Add chips and stir until dissolved. Spread over top of cake. Chill in refrigerator.

Lemon Cheesecake ... in three easy steps
LaVece Hughes

2 8-oz cream cheese
½ c sugar
1 T fresh lemon juice
½ t grated lemon peel

½ t vanilla
2 eggs
Graham cracker crust

Mix cream cheese, sugar, juice, peel and vanilla on medium speed until well blended. Add eggs; mix thoroughly. Pour into crust. Bake at 350 degrees for 30 minutes or until center is almost set. Cool. Refrigerate 3 hours or overnight.

Apple Pudding
LaVece Hughes

2 cups flour
2 t cinnamon
1 t salt
1 t baking soda
2 cups sugar

¼ cup butter
2 eggs
1 cup nuts (walnuts or pecans)
4 cups Granny Smith Apples

Mix dry ingredients together. Add remaining ingredients. Bake 40 minutes in an 11x13 in dish in a 350-degree oven. Serve with the sauce below and cool whip.

Sauce:
1 cup butter
2 t vanilla
2 cups sugar

1 cup Half and Half
pinch of nutmeg

Mix ingredients and cook 5 minutes in a double boiler. Do not boil.

"Wrinkles should merely indicate where smiles have been."
— Mark Twain

Chocolate Almond-Torte
Joan Tozer

1 pkg chocolate cake mix
1⅓ c slivered almonds
½ c sugar
1 small pkg vanilla instant pudding

1¼ c milk
¾ t almond extract
1½ c cool whip
1 tub prepared chocolate frosting

Heat oven to 350 degrees. Bake cake in two 9-inch pans as directed on pkg. Cool 10 minutes; remove from pans and cool completely. Split cake to make four layers. Cool almonds and sugar over medium heat, stirring constantly, until sugar is melted and almonds are coated. Spread on wax paper. Cool and break apart. Mix pudding, milk, and almond extract until smooth and well blended. Fold in cool whip. Spread ¼ of the pudding mixture and ¼ of the almonds between layers and on top of torte. Frost sides of torte with chocolate frosting. Refrigerate two to three hours before serving. Refrigerate remaining torte.

"Joan brought this to a church meeting one evening, and I have never seen so many men stand around and lick a cake plate like they did that night." — lgh

Chocolate Cake
Mary Barker from Ford's Favorite Recipes

Cake:
2 c sugar
2 c flour
½ c buttermilk
½ t soda
1 stick butter
½ c shortening
4 T cocoa
1 c water
2 eggs
1 t vanilla

Icing:
1 stick butter, melted
4 T cocoa
6 T milk

1 box powdered sugar
1 t vanilla
1 c chopped pecans

Sift sugar and flour together and stir in buttermilk, soda eggs and vanilla. In a saucepan mix butter, shortening, cocoa boil and water and bring to a boil. Pour over sugar-flour mixture and mix. Pour batter into a sheet cake pan and bake at 350 degrees for 35 minutes. Ice while still warm

To prepare icing bring milk, butter, and cocoa to a boil. Remove from heat and stir in powdered sugar, vanilla and pecans.

Chocolate Ice Box Dessert
Louise White from Leslie Webb

2 small pkg chocolate chips
2 T sugar
3 eggs, separated and beaten

1 c chopped nuts
1 pint whipping cream
1 large angel food cake

Melt chocolate chips and sugar in a double boiler and remove from heat. Stir in beaten egg yolks and let cool for 5 minutes.

Beat 3 egg whites until stiff. Fold in chopped nuts and whipping cream. Then fold into the chocolate mixture.

Crumble 1 large angel food cake and put half of the crumbs in a 9 x 12 rectangular pan. Pour half of the chocolate mixture over the cake. Add other layer of the cake crumbs and remaining chocolate mixture. Place in refrigerator to set. Serves 15.

Chocolate Pudding Cake
LaVece Hughes

1 c flour
¾ c sugar
1 T cocoa
2 t baking powder
¼ t salt
¾ chopped nuts

½ c milk
2 T melted butter
1 t vanilla
1 c brown sugar
¼ c cocoa
1 ¾ c boiling water

In a 9-inch square cake pan, mix together the flour, sugar, 2 T cocoa, baking powder, salt and nuts. Blend in the milk, melted butter and vanilla. In separate bowl, mix the brown sugar and the ¼ c cocoa and pour over the flour mixture in the pan. Pour boiling water over all. Bake at 350 degrees for 25 minutes. Makes 8-10 very rich servings.

I love this warm pudding cake; brownies on the top and chocolate pudding on the bottom. Even better with cool whip or ice cream

Coal Miner's Cake
LaVece Hughes

1 box Devil's Food cake mix
1 can cherry pie filling

2 eggs
1 t vanilla

Preheat oven to 350 degrees. Mix all ingredients and bake in a 9x13 pan for 30 to 35 minutes. While cake is still hot, cover with topping

Topping:
1 c sugar
1 stick margarine
¼ c evaporated milk

6 oz pkg chocolate chips
½ c pecans or walnuts, chopped

In saucepan, warm mixture of sugar, margarine and evaporated milk over low heat. Bring to low boil for one minute; add chocolate chips and nuts. Pour over cake.

Cream Cheese Pound Cake
Thelma Hatcher

1 c margarine, softened
½ c butter, softened (do not
        substitute)
8 oz cream cheese, softened

3 cups sugar
6 eggs
3 cups flour
2 t vanilla

Combine first 3 ingredients, creaming well. Gradually add sugar, beating until light and fluffy. Add eggs, one at a time, beating well after each addition. Add flour to creamed mixture, stirring until combined. Stir in vanilla. Pour batter into a well-greased 10-inch tube pan. Bake at 325 degrees for 1 hour and 45 minutes or until cake test done. Cool in pan 10 minutes, remove from pan, and cool completely.

Cupcakes . . . quick and easy
LaVece Hughes

1 pkg cake mix
1 8 oz cream cheese, softened

¼ c preserves
1 can of cake frosting

Make cake mix according to pkg directions. Fill 18 cup cakes, half the way up. Add dollop of creamed cheese and preserves mixed together. Cook for 325 degrees till done. Ice with can of frosting.

Dump Cake . . . never a bite left
LaVece Hughes

1 can cherry pie filling
8¼-oz can crushed pineapple,
    do not drain
1 yellow cake mix

2 sticks butter, melted
2½-oz can flaked coconut
1 c chopped pecans
Kool Whip for topping

Spoon cherry pie filling evenly in bottom of large sheet cake pan. Spread pineapple over cherry pie filling. Sprinkle dry cake mix over pineapple, then sprinkle coconut and finally pecans. Pour melted butter over the top and bake at 325 degrees for about 45 minutes until golden brown

Easy, quick, and very good. Can mix when beginning dinner and have ready in time for serving.

Flop Cake
LaVece Hughes

1 yellow cake mix
1 egg
1 stick butter, melted
8 oz cream cheese, softened

1 box powdered sugar
2 eggs
your favorite caramel frosting

Mix cake mix, one egg and butter together in a sheet cake pan. Spread evenly over bottom of pan. Mix cream cheese, powdered sugar and 2 eggs together with a blender and pour over mixture in pan. Bake at 350 degrees for 35 to 40 minutes. Frost cake with your favorite caramel frosting.

Fudge Cake . . . Soccer Mom style
LaVece Hughes

1 small pkg chocolate pudding
    (cook and serve kind)
2 c milk

1 box chocolate cake mix
1 c chocolate chips
½ c chopped nuts

Cook pudding and milk as directed on package. Blend dry cake mix into hot putting. Pour into 9 x 13 pan. Sprinkle chocolate chips and nuts on top. Bake 350 degrees for 30-35 minutes. Serve warm with Kool Whip.

German Chocolate Cake
LaVece Hughes

1 German chocolate cake mix

Icing:
⅔ c sugar
⅔ c evaporated milk
2 egg yolks, slightly beaten
⅓ c butter
½ t vanilla

1⅓ c flaked coconut
⅔-1 c chopped pecans

Prepare cake mix according to package directions and bake in two 8-inch pans. Cool cake. To make icing: Combine all except the coconut and nuts in a pan. Cook and stir constantly over medium heat about 10 minutes or until the egg thickens. Remove from heat and add coconut and pecans.

Never-Fail Chocolate Icing . . . a must-have recipe
Betty Cecil Hughes

1 c granulated sugar
½ c water
6 T cocoa
Pinch of salt

1 t vanilla
½ stick butter
1 box powdered sugar, or more

Mix and heat granulated sugar, water, cocoa and salt until it come to a boil. Boil for 1 minute only. Remove from heat and add butter and vanilla. Beat and gradually add enough powdered sugar until spreading consistency is reached. May add a touch of milk if icing becomes too hard or too thick.

Never-Fail Caramel Icing
Betty Cecil Hughes

May also make an excellent caramel icing from the above recipe by substituting brown sugar for white sugar and omitting the chocolate. This recipe will work for any amount as along as a 2:1 ratio of sugar to water is used.

"Praise loudly; correct softly."
— Catherine II

Lemon Pudding Cake
Charlie Dickinson from Inez Dickinson

5 level t flour
1 c sugar
3 T butter, softened or melted

1 c milk
¼ c lemon juice, 2 lemons
¼ t grated lemon rind
3 eggs, separated

Mix flour and sugar; work butter into flour mixture and cream. Beat egg yolks until thick and lemon colored. Add yolks and milk to creamed mixture. Mix. Add gradually lemon juice and rind, and mix carefully. Beat egg whites until stiff, but not dry; fold into mixture carefully. Pour into a greased 8- 9-inch baking dish. Set dish in a pan containing about one inch of hot water; place in 350 degree oven and bake about 35 minutes or until set. Serves six.

"Delicious . . . cake on top and lemon pudding on the bottom. I serve it warm." — *lgh*

Midnight Bliss Chocolate Cake . . . fantastic
Susan Spears Hughes

1 pkg devil's food cake mix
1 pkg Jell-O instant chocolate
    pudding mix
½ c General Mills International
    coffee (Mocha Swiss Powder)

4 eggs
½ c oil
8 oz sour cream
½ c water
12-oz pkg mini chocolate chips

Preheat oven 350 degrees. Grease Bundt Pan. Beat all ingredients except chocolate chips at low speed until moistened. Beat at medium speed for 2 minutes. Stir in Chocolate pieces. Bake 50-6- minutes until toothpick comes out clean. Cool in pan for 20 –30 minutes. Take out of pan and continue cooling. When completely cooled, sprinkle with powdered sugar.

Absolutely fantastic chocolate cake. Heavy and moist, doesn't last long at our house--one of my husband's favorites. — *lgh*

Punch Bowl Cake . . . great, quick and easy
Kathy Brussell

1 Jiffy cake mix, prepared
1 large vanilla pudding prepared
bananas
chopped nuts

1 can crushed pineapple, drained
1 can cherry pie filling
Kool Whip

Crumble prepared cake into a big, clear bowl. Layer rest of ingredients and cool.

Pineapple Upside Down Cake . . . the easy way
Willette Saunders and LaVece Hughes

2 T butter
1 Jiffy cake mix
Small can pineapple rings

1 c brown sugar
Maraschino cherries

Heat butter and brown sugar in a skillet on the stove until sugar is melted. Remove from heat and add pineapples and several cherries in the center of circles. Mix cake mix according to directions of package and pour in skillet. Bake at 350 degrees for 30 minutes

Mountain Dew Cupcakes
John Brandenburg

½ c chopped pecans for
    lining muffin cups
1 box yellow cake mix with
    pudding in the mix
1 box instant vanilla pudding

½ c Mountain Dew
½ c oil
½ c water
4 eggs

Line muffin tins with papers and sprinkle with pecans. Mix cake mix with rest of the ingredients and spoon into cups. Fill half way. Cook for 50-60 minutes at 350 degrees.

Icing:
1 stick butter
1¾ c sugar   ¼ c Mountain Dew   3½ oz coconut

Mix ingredients and bring to a boil. Boil for 2 minutes. Pour over cupcakes while warm.

Mountain Pudding Cake
Lelia Handy

Melt ¾ stick of butter in 13 x 9 cake pan in a 350-degree oven.

Make batter of:

1 c flour	1 large can peaches, sliced
1 c sugar	optional: ice cream
1 ½ t baking powder	
¼ t salt	
¾ c milk	

Mix quickly and pour batter into pan. Let cover bottom of pan. Pour peaches with juice over top of the batter. Bake at 350 degrees for about one hour. Last 5 minutes, butter top of cake and sprinkle with sugar. Serve as is, or with ice cream.

Can put this in the oven when you start dinner and it will be done by the time everything else is ready. Can do this with pie cherries, too. — lgh

Oatmeal Coconut Cake
Kate Ganter

1 c quick cooking oats	1½ c sifted flour
1 stick butter	1 t soda
1 c white sugar	½ t salt
1 c brown sugar	1 t nutmeg
2 eggs	1 t ground cloves
1 t cinnamon	

Pour 1¼ cup boiling water over 1 cup quick cooking oats and 1 stick butter. Let stand for 20 minutes.

Add remaining ingredients to oatmeal mixture and bake for 35 minutes at 350 degrees in a 1 x 13 inch Pyrex dish.

Topping:

½ c margarine	1 c coconut
1 c brown sugar	1 c nuts
3 T milk	

Pour over hot cake and put under broiler for 2 minutes or until lightly browned.

Twinkie Delight
Karen Campbell

1 box Twinkies
2 small boxes butter pecan
    Instant pudding

8 oz cool whip
1 Heath Bar candy bar, crushed

Cut Twinkies in half lengthwise and place in an 11 x 7 glass dish or pan. Make pudding as directed on box and pour over the Twinkies. Spread cool whip on top and top with crushed Heath Bar. Refrigerate. Serves 8 – 12.

Strawberry Cake
Kate Ganter

1 pkg white cake mix
4 eggs
1 pkg strawberry Jell-O

1 c oil
1 c drained frozen strawberries
    (save juice)

Pour all but berries in mixer bowl and beat about 4 minutes. Add berries. Pour into large Pyrex casserole dish. Bake for 35 minutes at 325 degrees

Frosting:
¾ stick margarine
strawberry juice

1 box powdered sugar

Mix butter and sugar and as much liquid as need to make spreading consistency.

Pumpkin Roll
Sandy Godecker

Beat: 3 eggs and add 1 cup sugar and 1 teaspoon lemon juice.
Combine the following and fold into eggs;

1 t soda	1 t allspice
¼ t salt	½ t nutmeg
1 t ginger	¾ c flour

Add 2/3 cup pumpkin and stir.

Grease a cookie sheet with a lip with Pam and line with wax paper and
grease the waxed paper again. Spread the batter. Bake for 20 minutes at
350 degrees or until slightly browned. Turn out on a towel covered with
powdered sugar and remove waxed paper from back. Roll up long ways
with the towel in a jellyroll manner. Cool in the towel for 2 hours. Unroll,
and spread with filling; re-roll without the towel.

Filling:
1 c powdered sugar	¼ c soft margarine
8 oz cream cheese	2 t vanilla

Wrap in waxed paper and then in Reynolds Wrap. Refrigerate and slice as
needed. Freezes well.

*"This is great and everyone loves it. We use it for breakfast. It takes quite a
bit of preparation, but it is well worth it."— lgh*

*The object of teaching a child is to enable the child
to get along without the teacher.*

*"Life is like a snow bank, but to tell you the truth, I've been
drifting a little lately." — W.C. Fields*

Rum Cake
Mary Brock

½ c chopped pecans
1   Duncan Hines Butter Recipe
    Golden Cake Mix
1 small pkg vanilla instant pudding

4 eggs
½ c water
½ c oil
½ c light rum

Grease and flour a bundt pan. Crumble nuts in bottom of pan. Place cake mix and pudding mix in large bowl. Add rum, water, oil and eggs. Mix for six minutes. Pour batter into can pan and bake 50 –60 minutes at 325 degrees. Remove from oven and immediately pour on hot glaze. Let cool in bundt pan until it is completely cool. Wrap tightly.

Hot Glaze:
1 c sugar
1 stick butter
¼ c light rum
¼ c water

Mix ingredients, boil 2-3 minutes
and pour over cake

Woodford Pudding
Mary McMurray

½ c butter
1 c sugar
1 c flour
1 c blackberry jam

1 t baking powder
½ c milk
1 t cinnamon
3 eggs, beaten

Cream butter and sugar; add eggs. Add flour sifted with cinnamon and baking powder to the sugar and egg mixture along with the milk. Blend in the jam. Bake in greased dish about 8 x 12 for 40 minutes at 325 degrees.

Caramel Sauce:
1½ c brown sugar
Dash salt

1 c boiling water
4 T flour

Blend sugar, salt and flour and add boiling water in a sauce pan. Stir and cool 6-8 minutes. If too thick, may add more water. Take off of stove and add 4 T butter and ½ t vanilla.

Cookies

Apple Cookies . . . one of my favorites
Kate Ganter

½ c shortening
1⅓ c brown sugar
1 unbeaten egg
2 c flour
1 t soda
½ t salt
1 t cinnamon

½ t nutmeg
1 c chopped nuts
1 c finely chopped un-pared
    tart apples
1 c raisins
¼ c apple juice or milk

Let raisins stand in hot water until ready to use, then strain. Cream shortening and sugar. Add egg and mix well. Sift dry ingredients and add to mixture. Fold in apples, raisins and nuts. Add juice or milk and mix well. Drop by teaspoons on greased cookie sheet and bake at 350 degrees.

Glaze:
Mix together 1½ c sifted powdered sugar, 1T soft butter, ¼ t vanilla, ⅛ t salt and 2½ T milk.

Blackberry-Sage Thumbprints
LaVece Hughes

2 c flour
⅔ c cornmeal
1½ t dried sage, crushed
¼ t baking powder
1 c butter, softened

1 c packed brown sugar
2 egg yolks
2 t finely shredded lemon peel
1½ t vanilla
¾ c blackberry preserves

Mix flour, cornmeal, sage and baking powder. Set aside. In a large mixing bowl beat butter for 30 seconds with an electric mixer. Add sugar while mixing until combined. Mix in egg yolks, lemon peel, and vanilla. Mix in as much of the flour mixture as possible with the mixer. Stir in any remaining flour mixture. Pinch and roll dough into ¾-inch balls. Place balls one inch apart on an un-greased cookie sheet. With the tip of your thumb indent the top of each ball. Fill the indentation with about ¼ teaspoon of blackberry preserves. Bake about 10 minutes at 350 degrees or until the bottoms are lightly browned. Cool

Chocolate Chip Cheese Bars
Charlie Hughes

1 pkg (18 oz) refrigerated chocolate
    chip cookie dough
½ c sugar

1 egg
1 pkg (8 oz) cream cheese,
softened

Cut cookie dough in half. For crust, press half of the dough into the bottom of a greased 7-x11 inch baking pan. In a mixing bowl, beat cream cheese, sugar and egg until smooth. Spread over crust. Crumble remaining dough over top. Bake at 350 degrees for 40 minutes or until a toothpick inserted near the center comes out clean. Cool on rack. Refrigerate, if there are any leftovers.

"Even I can make this easy dessert ."

Chocolate Peanut Bars
Matt Hughes from Sue Thomas

1 pkg white cake mix
1⅓ c peanut butter
    (divided)
1 egg
8 oz cream cheese, softened

⅓ c milk
¼ c sugar
1 c chocolate chips
¾ c salted peanuts

In a mixing bowl, beat the cake mix, 1 c peanut butter and egg until crumbly. Press into a greased 13 x 9 baking dish. In a mixing bowl, combine cream cheese and remaining peanut butter. . Gradually beat in milk and sugar. Carefully spread over crust. Sprinkle with chocolate chips and peanuts. Bake at 350 degrees for 25-30 minutes or until edges are lightly browned and center is set. Cool completely before cutting. Store in the refrigerator. Yield 2 ½ dozen

Chocolate-Coconut Cookies
Tammy Jones

1 box chocolate cake mix
1 c flaked coconut

2 eggs
½ c oil

Mix all ingredients together. Pour mixture into a greased and floured 15 x 10 inch pan. Bake at 350 degrees for 15-20 minutes. Cool and cut into squares.

Fudge Brownies

Inez Dickinson

1 stick butter
1 c sugar
1 16-oz can Hershey's syrup
3 large or 4 small eggs

1¼ c flour
½ t vanilla
½ c chopped nuts
⅛ t salt

Cream margarine and sugar, add eggs and beat, add chocolate syrup, vanilla and flour and mix well. Add nuts last. Bake at 350 degrees in greased 13 x 9 Pyrex dish for 25 minutes. Caution - Do not overcook. Cool in pan for a few minutes. Spread with icing.

Icing:
6 T margarine
6 T milk
1⅓ c sugar
1 T white Karo syrup

1 c chocolate chips
½ c chopped pecans

Place margarine, milk, sugar, and syrup in saucepan and bring to full boil. Boil 1 minute, remove from heat and add chocolate chips. Stir till chips melt, add nuts, and then pour quickly over brownies and spread

Microwave Brownies

LaVece Hughes

⅔ c margarine
1 c sugar
2 eggs, slightly beaten
1 t vanilla
1 c sifted flour

¼ c cocoa
¼ c instant cocoa mix
½ t baking powder
½ c chopped nuts

Melt margarine in bowl on high for one minute or until melted. Add sugar. Cool. Add eggs, and vanilla. Sift flour, dry cocoa, instant cocoa and baking powder into sugar mixture and blend in. Stir in nuts. Pour into lightly greased 9 inch baking dish. Cook on high in microwave for 4 ½ to 5 ½ minutes. Cool before cutting.

Almost as good as Aunt Inez's, and quicker.

> *"To be an adopted child means you grew in your mother's head and not in her stomach."* — Steve Drew

Coffee and Spice Drops
Thelma Hatcher

1 c soft shortening	3½ cups flour
2 c brown sugar	1 t soda
2 eggs	1 t salt
	1 t nutmeg
½ c cold coffee.	1 t cinnamon
	raisins and nuts (optional)

Mix first three ingredients thoroughly, then stir in the cold coffee. Stir in remaining ingredients from second column. Chill at least one hour. Drop rounded teaspoonfuls about 2 inches apart on lightly greased baking sheet. Bake until set, when touched lightly with finger leaves no imprint. Cook at 400 degrees for 8-10 minutes. Makes 6 dozen

Blonde Brownies
LaVece Hughes

⅔ c oil	2 c flour
2 c brown sugar, packed	1 T salt
2 eggs	¼ t baking soda
2 T water	1 t baking powder
½ c nuts	2 t vanilla
	6 oz chocolate chips

Mix all ingredients except chocolate chips and spread in a 10 x 14 inch pan. Sprinkle chocolate chips on top and bake at 350 degrees for about 30 minutes or until done.

Chess Cookies . . . yummy
Emmy Lou Dickinson, from Our Cousin's Kitchen

1 Duncan Hines yellow cake mix	2 eggs, well beaten
1 stick butter, softened	8 oz cream cheese
1 egg	1 16-oz box powdered sugar

Blend cake mix, butter and 1 egg. Press into a 9 x 13 inch baking dish. Blend beaten eggs, cream cheese and sugar until smooth. Pour over pressed mixture and bake at 350 degrees for 35-40 minutes.

Coconut Chews ... an oldie, but goodie
LaVece Hughes from Kate Ganter

⅔ c margarine
1½ c brown sugar
1 c sifted flour
½ t salt
2 eggs

1 t baking powder
1 t vanilla
1 c coconut
¾ c nuts, more or less

Melt margarine in large pan; blend in sugar. Sift flour, salt and baking powder. Combine all ingredients with the brown sugar mixture. Bake in a greased and floured 11 x 7 inch pan for 25-30 minutes at 350 degrees.

Death-by-Chocolate Cookies
LaVece Hughes

2 8-oz pkg Baker's semi sweet
    chocolate, or summer coating
¾ c firmly packed brown sugar
¼ c margarine

2 eggs
1 t vanilla
½ c flour
¼ t baking powder
2 c chopped pecans

Heat oven to 350 degrees. Coarsely chop half of the chocolate (8 squares); set aside. Microware remaining 8 squares chocolate in large bowl on high 1 –2 minutes. Stir until chocolate is melted and smooth. Stir in sugar, butter, eggs and vanilla. Stir in flour and baking powder. Stir in reserved chopped chocolate and nuts. Drop by ¼ cupfuls onto an un-greased cookie sheet. Bake 12-13 minutes or until cookies rise and are set to the touch. Cool on cookie sheet for one minute. Transfer to waxed paper. Makes 15-20 cookies.

Cranberry Crispies ... from a bread mix
LaVece Hughes

1 pkg (15.6 oz) cranberry quick
    bread mix
½ c melted margarine

½ c chopped walnuts or pecans
1 egg
½ c dried cranberries

Combine bread mix, butter, nuts, and egg; Stir in cranberries. Roll into 1-1/4 in balls. Place on ungreased cookie sheet. Flatten to 1/8 in thick with a glass dipped in sugar. Bake at 350 degrees for 10-12 minutes until lightly browned. Makes 2½ dozen.

Egg Kisses . . . an old and very good recipe
LaVece Hughes from Mary Withers Snyder

3 large egg whites
1 c sugar
¼ t cream of tartar

1 t vanilla
¾ c chocolate chips
½ c chopped nuts

Beat egg whites, vanilla, and cream of tartar in large glass bowl until foamy. Gradually add sugar and beat until stiff. Add chocolate chips and nuts. Drop by teaspoonful onto on 2 cookie sheets lined with large brown paper bags. (Do not grease bags) Cook for 1 hour at 275 degrees. Turn off oven and don't open door until cool. *Works best if let sit in oven overnight.*

Mary Wither's Egg Kisses are one of the very best cookies I have ever eaten. — lgh

Graham Cracker Cookies
Ann Burns

Melt and boil for 3 minutes:
1 c margarine
1 c brown sugar
½ t cinnamon

Pour sugar mixture over:
2 pkgs separated graham crackers on a deep-lipped cookie sheet.

Sprinkle with 2 cups chopped nuts and bake for 10 minutes at 400 degrees. Remove immediately and put onto waxed paper.

"Great and the quickest cookie you can make." — lgh

Lemon Angel Bars
LaVece Hughes

1-lb box, one-step Angel Food Cake Mix
21-oz can prepared lemon pie filling

Preheat oven to 350 degrees. Mix the two ingredients together and pour into an un-greased 10½ x 15½ inch jellyroll pan. Bake for 20 to 25 minutes. Cool and cut into 24 squares.

If you focus on results, you will never change. If you focus on change you will get results. — Susan Sallee

Hello Dolly Cookies
Kate Ganter

Melt 2 T margarine in a 9 x 11 pan. Then sprinkle the following in layers:

1½ c graham cracker crumbs (roll about 18 crackers yourself;
    the packaged kind doesn't work as well here)
1 c angel flake coconut
1 c chocolate chips
1 c butterscotch chips
1 c chopped nuts

Pour one can of sweetened condensed milk over the top, evenly. Bake at 350 degrees for 20-30 minutes, and then cool thoroughly before cutting into squares.

This is one of our family's favorite cookies. — lgh

Knock-Your-Socks-Off Brownies
LaVece Hughes

1 pkg German chocolate cake mix
1 c chopped nuts
⅓ c + ½ c evaporated milk, divided
½ c melted butter
60 vanilla caramels (14 oz pkg)
1 c chocolate chips

In a large mixing bowl, combine dry cake mix, nuts, ⅓ cup evaporated milk and melted butter. Press half of the batter into the bottom of a greased 13 x 9 inch glass-baking dish. Bake in a preheated 350-degree oven for 8 minutes.

In the microwave melt caramels with remaining ½ cup evaporated milk. When caramel mixture is well mixed, pour over baked layer. Cover with chocolate chips. Chill for about an hour or until the caramel is hard. Press the remaining batter on top of morsels. Return to oven and bake 28 minutes (or less for gooier brownies). Cool before cutting.

*"I have never killed anyone, but I have read many
obituaries with pleasure." — Clarence Darrell*

Lemon Bars
LaVece Hughes

Crust:
1 c flour
⅓ c softened margarine
¼ c powdered sugar

Topping:
1 c sugar
2 c flour
½ t lemon extract
½ t baking powder
2 eggs
2 T lemon juice
¼ t salt

Combine crust and pat into 8-inch square baking pan. Bake 375 for 15 minutes, meanwhile, combine sugar, eggs, flour, lemon juice, extract, baking powder, and salt in mixing bowl. Mix until frothy. Pour over crust. Bake 375 degrees for 18–22 minutes or until golden brown. Dust with powdered sugar.

No-Bake Chocolate Cookies
Ed Hughes from My Grandmother Betty Hughes

Mix and boil for 2 minutes:
2 c sugar
⅓ c cocoa
½ t vanilla

½ c milk
1 stick margarine

Remove from heat and add:
3 c uncooked oatmeal
½ c peanut butter

Mix together well. May also add ½ cup raisins. Drop by teaspoonful onto waxed paper.

Cookie or candy? Very quick and very good. — lgh

"Smart Kids or Smart Bombs? Put your money where your future is."
—Bumper Sticker

Oatmeal Cookies . . . best oatmeal cookie ever
Selma Dickinson

1 c shortening
2 c brown sugar, packed
2 eggs
1 T vinegar
1½ c flour
⅓ t salt

2 t baking powder
1 T cinnamon
½ c chopped nuts
½ c raisins
2 c oatmeal

Cream shortening and sugar. Add vinegar, add eggs, and beat well after each addition. Add flour sifted, salt, baking powder and cinnamon. Add raisins, nuts and oatmeal. Bake for 10 minutes at 375 degrees.

Vinegar is the secret to these delicious cookies. Aunt Selma's niece, Mary Lynn, suggests adding a cup of chocolate chips to this recipe. — lgh

Oatmeal Cookies . . . another winner
LaVece Hughes

1 c butter or margarine, melted
2 eggs
1 c white sugar
1 box vanilla instant pudding
¾ c firmly packed brown sugar
1 t soda

pinch of salt
1¼ c of flour
½ c pecans
1 c raisins
1 t vanilla
3½ c quick cook oats

Cream butter, sugar, soda, salt, and egg. Add vanilla, flour, raisins, pudding and nuts until smooth. Add oats last. Drop from spoon onto ungreased baking sheet about 2 inches apart. Bake at 375 degrees for 9 minutes.

According to Jeff Foxworthy, "You might be a Redneck if you think a Quarter Horse is the horse out in front of Wal-Mart."

Pecan Sundies

Patsy Alexander Nielsen

1 c butter	1 t vanilla
⅓ c sugar	2 c flour (sifted)
2 t water	1 c chopped pecans

Mix butter and sugar. Add water and vanilla and mix well. Add flour and pecans. Chill if time permits. Shape into walnut sized balls and bake on an un-greased cookie sheet at 325 degrees for 20 minutes. Cool slightly and roll in powdered sugar.

This is a favorite old-time recipe. Magee's Bakery in Lexington makes a similar cookie, but flattens it down to cook, and instead of rolling it in the powdered sugar, places a dollop of colored powder sugar icing on top when it is baked. — lgh

Peanut Butter 'n' Fudge Bars . . . a real winner

Fran Jones

2 c firmly packed brown sugar	¼ t salt, optional
1 c butter, softened	2 c Quaker oats
¼ c plus 2 T peanut butter, divided	14-oz can sweetened condensed milk
2 eggs	12 oz chocolate chips
2 c flour	⅔ c chopped peanuts
1 t baking soda	

Heat oven to 350 degrees. Grease 13 x 9 inch baking pan. In large mixing bowl, beat brown sugar, butter and ¼ c peanut butter until light and fully. Beat in eggs. Add combined four, baking soda and salt; beat until well mixed. Stir in oats; mix well. Reserve 1 c of oat mixture; set aside. Spread remaining oat mixture evenly. In a small saucepan, combine milk, chocolate chips, and remaining 2 T peanut butter. Cook over low heat until chocolate is melted, stirring constantly. Remove from heat; stir in peanuts. Spread mixture evenly over crust in pan. Drop remaining oat mixture by teaspoonfuls evenly over chocolate mixture. Bake 25 to 30 minutes or until light golden brown. Cool completely on wire. Cut into bars. Makes 32 bars.

It's difficult to soar with the Eagles when you run with Turkeys!

Pumpkin Bars
LaVece Hughes

2 c flour
2 t baking powder
1 t baking soda
½ t salt
2 t cinnamon
4 eggs

15-oz can pumpkin
1⅔ c sugar
1 c oil
1 c chopped pecans
1 recipe cream cheese frosting, below

Combine flour, baking powder, soda, salt and cinnamon; set aside. In a mixing bowl, beat together eggs, pumpkin, sugar and oil. Add flour mixture; beat well. Stir in pecans. Spread in an un-greased 15 x 10 baking dish. Bake in 350-degree oven for 25-30 minutes. Cool on wire rack, then frost with icing below and sprinkle chopped pecans on top. Cut into 24 bars.

Cream Cheese Icing:
3 oz pkg cream cheese, softened
¼ c margarine

1 t vanilla
2 c powdered sugar

In a bowl, beat together softened cream cheese, margarine and vanilla until fluffy. Gradually add powdered sugar, beating until smooth.

Rum Brownies . . . easy and good
Jeanne White

1 brownie mix, with nuts or
     add ½ c nuts
2 cups powdered sugar
rum

1 t milk
1 t butter
6 oz chocolate chips

Make brownies according to directions on box. Cool. Add milk and butter to powdered sugar and enough rum to make easy to spread over brownies. Melt chocolate chips in microwave in a measuring cup on 50% power for 2 minutes. Stir until melted and drizzle in strings on top of rum icing.

If cookies get hard in a cookie jar, don't toss them out; a piece of bread in the container will soften them almost immediately. — Jean Glasier

Peanut Butterscotches
Thelma Hatcher

2⅓ c flour
1 c shortening
1 c sugar
½ c brown sugar
1 c peanuts
1 t soda

1 pkg butterscotch morsels
1 t salt
2 eggs
1 t vanilla
⅔ c raisins

Sift flour, baking soda, and salt. Cream shortening, add sugar gradually and cream until fluffy. Add eggs and vanilla and mix well. Add sifted dry ingredients and mix well. Add peanuts, raisins and butterscotch morsels. Drop by spoonfuls on greased cookie sheets. Cook for 15 minutes at 350 degrees.

Pecan Pie Bars
LaVece Hughes

Filling:
3 large eggs
¾ c corn syrup
¾ c sugar
2 T butter, melted
1 t vanilla
11½ oz chocolate chips
1½ c chopped pecans

Crust:
1½ c flour
1 stick butter, softened
¼ c packed brown sugar

Crust:
Beat flour, butter and brown sugar in small mixing bowl until crumble. Press into a greased 13 x 9 Pyrex pan. In an oven preheated to 350 degrees, bake for 12-15 minutes or until lightly browned.

Filling:
Beat eggs, corn syrup, sugar, butter and vanilla in medium bowl with wire whisk. Stir in chips and nuts. Pour evenly over baked crust. Bake for 25-30 minutes or until set. Cool in the pan on a wire rack.

If you want your bar cookies to be crisp on the bottom, use a metal pan, not a glass pan. Glass pans make bars soft on the bottom and they often stick.

Scotcheroos
Mary McMurray

Bring to a boil:
1 c sugar
1 c karo syrup

Add:
6-7 c Rice Crispies
1 c peanut butter

Mix and spread in a buttered 9 x 13 inch pan.

Melt and spread over top:
6 oz chocolate chips
6 oz butterscotch chips

Snickerdoodles
LaVece Hughes

½ c margarine
½ c shortening
2½ c sugar
2 eggs

2½ c flour
1 t soda
2 t cream of tartar
1½ t salt

Cream margarine, shortening and sugar. Add eggs and blend. Sift dry ingredients and add to creamed mixture. Chill, if time permits, and shape into walnut sized balls. Roll in colored Christmas sugars or a sugar and cinnamon mixture. Place 2" apart on an un-greased cookie sheet and bake at 350 degrees for 16 minutes. Makes 4 dozen.

This crisp and chewy cookie has replaced Christmas Sugar Cookies at our house and is much easier to prepare. We always double this recipe. — lgh

Brownie S'Mores

LaVece Hughes

1 large (19-21 oz) pkg brownie mix
3 eggs
2 cups little marshmallows

6 T butter
¼ cup milk
12 whole Graham crackers

Prepare brownie mix according to directions and bake in a 325-degree oven until done, about 25 minutes. A toothpick should come out fairly clean from the middle. Sprinkle the marshmallows on the top of the brownies and cover with the graham crackers as soon as they come out of the oven. Bake for 2 more minutes and remove the pan from the oven. Press the graham crackers down into the marshmallows. Cool on a wire rack and then turn out upside down. Invert and cut into graham cracker squares.

Oatmeal Caramel Bars

Susan Sallee

Bars:
2 c flour
2 c quick-cooking rolled oats
1½ c firmly packed brown sugar
1 t baking soda
1¼ c margarine or butter, softened
½ t salt

Filling:
3 T flour
½ c nuts
6 oz chocolate chips
12½-oz jar caramel ice cream topping

Heat oven to 350 degrees. Grease 13 x 9 pan. In large bowl, combine all bar ingredients; mix at low speed until crumbly. Reserve half of crumb mixture (about 3 cups) for topping. Press remaining crumb mixture in bottom of greased pan. Bake at 350 degrees for 10 minutes. In a small bowl, combine caramel topping and 3 T of flour. Remove partially baked bars from oven; sprinkle with chocolate chips and nuts. Drizzle evenly with caramel mixture; sprinkle with reserved crumb mixture. Bake at 350 degrees for an additional 18-22 minutes or until golden brown. Cool. May refrigerate to set filling.

"You are not given the keys to salvation.
You find them for yourself."
— Martin Luther

Salted Peanut Chews . . . like a Payday candy bar
Patsy Alexander Nielsen

Preheat oven to 350 degrees and mix until crumbly.

First layer
1½ c flour   ½ t baking powder
¼ t soda   ½ t salt
⅔ c brown sugar, pressed   ½ c softened butter
2 egg yolks   1 t vanilla

Press into a 13 x 9 Pyrex pan and bake for 15 minutes.

Second layer
Add 3 cups miniature marshmallows and bake 3-4 more minutes. Remove from oven.

Third layer
10 oz peanut butter chips   ⅔ c karo syrup
¼ c butter   2 t vanilla

Cook over low heat until melted and smooth. Add
2 cup Rice Krispies
2 cup salted peanuts

Pour over second layer and allow to cool.

"Education's purpose is to replace an empty mind with an open one."
— *Malcolm Forbes*

Cinnamon Christmas Ornaments . . . <u>not for eating</u>
LaVece Hughes

cinnamon
applesauce

Combine equal amounts of cinnamon and apple sauce and roll very thin
on wax paper. Sprinkle lightly with cinnamon. Cut with holiday shaped
cookie cutters. Use a straw to poke a small hole in the top of the
ornament. Place on cookie sheets and bake in a 200-degree oven for 1 to
1 ½ hours. Let cool; put a ribbon through the top to hang.

Drinks

Easy Cocoa Mix
LaVece Hughes

2-lb box Nestlé's Quik
16-oz jar Coffee-mate

1-lb box powdered sugar
8-oz box dry milk

Mix all ingredients together well. Store in an airtight container. Use 3-4 heaping tablespoons of mix per cup of boiling water. Top with cool whip.

Cranberry Punch
LaVece Hughes

1 qt cranberry juice cocktail
1 qt pineapple juice
¼ c sugar

2 t almond extract
2 liters (or qts) ginger ale, chilled

Combine first four ingredients, stirring until sugar dissolves. Cover and chill at least four hours. To serve, pour juice mixture into punch bowl and stir in ginger ale.

Boiled Drinking Custard
Jeanne White from My Grandmother Lucy Goodman

1 half-gallon whole milk
6 eggs

¾ to 1 c sugar
Vanilla

Heat milk until it gets a skim on top. Beat eggs with mixer. Add sugar and beat well. Add some hot milk to egg mixture. Add mixture to heated milk gradually, stirring constantly. Cook until custard thickens and coats a metal spoon. Stir mixture continuously. Remove from heat. Optional: Strain custard through gauze cloth. Add vanilla, and 1 ½ teaspoon or to taste. Refrigerate and serve with dollop of whipped cream and sprinkle of nutmeg.

This old recipe is still great and is best when made the day before serving.

Bourbon Slush . . . the St. Louie way

Jennie Lee Werremeyer

2 6-oz orange juice
2 6-oz lemonade
Bourbon

9 c water
1 T instant tea
1¾ c sugar

Freeze in a plastic container. Mix frozen slush half and half with 7-up or favorite clear soda.

Bourbon Slush . . . Liz's Party Pleaser

Liz Moore

2 tea bags
1 c boiling water
1 c sugar
3½ cups of cold water

6-oz can of orange juice, thawed
½ c bourbon
6 oz frozen lemonade, thawed
2 6-oz cans frozen limeade

Mix tea and boiling water and seep for 3-4 minutes. Stir in sugar. Stir in rest. Freeze until firm. Thaw until it "slushes". Serve "as is."

Vodka Slush . . . makes 2 batches

Liz Moore

2 6-oz cans frozen lemonade
1 6-oz can frozen orange juice
2 6-oz cans frozen limeade

Thaw the frozen juices, but not completely, and stir in 3½ cans of water

Add 1-cup sugar (or more if your taste requires) and 2 cups of vodka, mix and freeze for at least 24 hours. When you serve, fill cup approximately ¾ full of your brew and top off with 7-up or Sprite.

Signs on Church Marquee:
— God responds to Knee Mail.
— Home repair center,

Grape Wine

LaVece Hughes

40 oz Welch's grape juice	1-gallon jug
4½ c sugar	1 large balloon (10 c size)
½ t dry yeast	1 qt water

Pour grape juice into a narrow neck jug. Mix sugar and yeast in saucepan and add 1 qt warm water to dissolve sugar. Pour into jug. Fill rest of jug with warm water and mix well. Stretch neck of balloon over top of jug. Set out of sunlight for 21 days. Balloon will gradually grow.

Remove balloon and drink ¼ of contents; find a soft spot to fall. — lgh

Orange Julius

LaVece Hughes

1 c orange juice	½ c dry milk powder
1½ T sugar	½ t vanilla
½ c ice	1 scoop vanilla ice cream

Blend in blender until ice is crushed.

Peach Tea

Molly Ann Showalter and Jack Larson
Labrot and Graham Distillery

Dilute 1 quart of Tetley Peach Tea concentrate to 2 gallons with cold water. Serve "on the rocks."

"This tea was served recently after a tour of the Distillery and it is really fantastic, and couldn't be easier. My husband said, "What kind of recipe is this?" I told him, "That, my dear, is one even you can prepare." — lgh

"I haven't spoken to my wife for 18 month. I hate to interrupt her"
Tom and Ray Magliozzi (aka National Public Radio's
Click and Clack –The Tappet Brothers)

Tea Punch

Selma Dickinson from Elsie Crouch

2 c boiling water
1 c sugar
7 tea bags

12 oz frozen orange juice
12 oz frozen lemonade
water to make 1 gallon

Steep tea bags in boiling water for 3 minutes. Add sugar and the rest of ingredients.

This is a yummy family favorite for summer get-togethers and we refer to it as Aunt Selma's Punch.— lgh

Wedding Punch

Diane Crossfield from Kathy Crossfield

4 c sugar
6 c water
46 oz pineapple juice

12 oz frozen lemonade
12 oz frozen orange juice
6 bananas

Combine all ingredients; puree bananas in blender with small amount of juice. Mix all together and pour into 2-3 gallon size freezer bag and freeze over night. Place a frozen bag of punch into bowl and pour 2 liters of ginger ale over slush.

My wife and I go out to dinner and a movie every week . . .
She goes on Tuesdays and I go on Fridays.
Tom and Ray Magliozzi (aka National
Public Radio's Click and Clack—
The Tappet Brothers)

Candies

Black Walnut Candy . . . a very old recipe
Kate Ganter from Hattie Rogers

2 c brown sugar
1½ c black walnuts
1 lump butter

1 c milk
1 t Karo syrup (optional)

Put sugar, milk and karo on to cook and stir every now and then to keep from curdling. As soon as it starts to boil, add butter. When a few drops of the candy forms a soft ball in cold water, remove from fire and add walnuts. Let cool before beating. When thick and creamy, drop by spoonfuls on buttered dish or waxed paper.

Brown Sugar Fudge
LaVece Hughes

¼ c margarine
1 c brown sugar
1 c white sugar

¾ c sour cream
1 t vanilla
½ c chopped walnuts

Melt butter in heavy saucepan. Add brown sugar and heat to boiling. Add sugar and sour cream. Cook over medium heat until sugar dissolves, then allow mixture to rise to a slightly higher heat of 236 degrees, without stirring. Cool at room temperature to lukewarm. Beat until mixture holds its shape and loses its gloss. Quickly add vanilla and nuts. Spread immediately in a buttered 8 in square pan. Makes about 50 pieces.

Candy is cooked to the soft-ball stage when a few drops of the candy dropped into cup of cold water can be, using your fingers, formed into a soft ball. Don't touch the candy while it's hot—it's very hot.

"A mother is a person who, seeing that there are only four pieces of pie for five people, promptly announces she never did care for pie."
-- Source Unknown

Bourbon Balls . . . none better

LaVece Hughes

2 c chopped pecans
Bourbon to cover chopped nuts
2 boxes (at least) powdered sugar

1 stick margarine
1-2 lb <u>dark</u> chocolate summer coating

Soak chopped pecans in enough bourbon to cover. Soak as long as possible, more than 24 hours of soaking makes better candy. Pour off bourbon and save. Mix powdered sugar and margarine with enough of the bourbon from the nuts to make a doughy mixture in a large bowl with an electric mixer. Use more or less sugar and bourbon to make the right consistency to work with your hands. Add the drained nuts and mix well. (May need more sugar after adding nuts.) Roll into small balls and place on waxed paper on cookie sheets. Carefully melt the summer coating a pound at a time in a pan on the stove-top (warm setting), stirring often. Caution-- too much heat will cause the summer coating to burn. Hand dip each piece with the thumb and middle finger. Shake off excess and allow to dry on wax paper. Makes about 100 pieces.

"Summer coating lacks cocoa butter and is easily melted. It comes in all kinds of flavors and may be purchased in many candy stores and in some groceries. Most who try these tell me they are better than Rebecca Ruth's. The real secret to this recipe though, is to soak the nuts." — *lgh*

Coconut Bonbons

LaVece Hughes

2½ cups dry coconut, finely shredded
¾ c white Karo syrup
summer coating, your choice of flavors

Heat Karo syrup to just before it boils and mix in coconut. Let sit for a while to cool. Shape into about 50 balls. You may need to clean hands and leave them wet periodically. Dip in summer coating. *(I use green coating for coconut bonbons. My husband says to skip the green or white stuff and go straight for the dark semi-sweet chocolate coating which he says is far superior—the result is similar to a Mounds candy bar.)*

Peanut Butter Balls
LaVece Hughes

Small jar of crunchy peanut butter
1 stick margarine, softened
1 lb powdered sugar

Mix ingredients, gradually adding the powdered sugar until dough like consistency. Roll into grape sized balls and dip in summer coating.

Butterscotch Party Mix
Kim Overstreet

2 c Chex cereal
2 c small pretzel twists
1 c dry roasted peanuts

20 caramels (quartered)
1 pkg butterscotch chips (11 oz)

Mix the cereal, pretzels, peanuts and caramels. Melt the butterscotch chips in the microwave at 70% for 1 minute. Continue at 10-20 second intervals until smooth. Pour over cereal mixture and pour out on to waxed paper to harden. Once hardened, break apart.

I sprinkle colorful candies into mixture before it hardens. Red and Green M&Ms for Christmas, candy corn for Halloween, pastel M&Ms in the spring...whatever I have.

"This is so good and goes so quickly, I always double Kim's recipe." — lgh

Christmas Fudge . . . the old fashioned way
Kate Ganter from Lelia Rogers Dickinson

2 c sugar
½ c cocoa
1 lump butter

⅔ c milk
¼ c white corn syrup
1 t vanilla

Mix cocoa and sugar; add milk, corn syrup, and butter. Cook and stir until it makes a firm ball when dropped in cold water. Cool and add vanilla and beat well until it as firm enough to handle. Butter hands and gather it into large lump and knead well. Pinch off small pieces and roll into balls with buttered hands. Decorate with pecan halves, candied cherries, chopped nuts or coconuts.

"This is a good old time recipe and Kate would always double this recipe at Christmas."

Chocolate Cream Mints . . . easy and yummy

LaVece Hughes

3 oz cream cheese
2¼ cups confectioner's sugar
chocolate summer coating

Combine cheese and sugar and pinch off pieces of the dough, roll into balls and roll in granulated sugar. (You can flavor the dough with any oil flavorings such as cherry, strawberry, lemon, peppermint, etc. but they are good plain, too. They also freeze well for later use. Place dough balls on wax paper on a cookie sheet or tray; flatten with fork and let dry. Then dip in summer coating.

These may be dipped in any flavor summer coating. Don't roll them in granulated sugar, though. I adapted the recipe for these mints from a recipe by Debbie Jenkins Cook who writes a weekly column for the Harrodsburg Herald. *Her column is easily worth the cost of the newspaper. I added the final touch—the chocolate coating.*

Date-Nut Loaf . . . an old, family treasure

Kate Ganter from Hattie Rogers

2 c white sugar
1 c sweet milk
1 T butter

1 box dates, chopped
1 c chopped nuts

Boil sugar and mix, stirring occasionally until softball stage. Then add dates and boil 5 minutes longer. Add nuts and butter and boil a few minutes longer. Place pan in cold water to cool. When cool, beat with spoon until firm enough to handle. Roll on marble top or waxed paper or other smooth surface into two long narrow rolls. Wrap rolls in waxed paper and put in cool place. After several hours or next day, slice into rounds.

When making chocolate cake, use cocoa instead of flour to coat your cake pan. This will keep the cake from having white-flour "dust" on it when you remove it from the pan.

Fannie Farmer's Chocolate Fudge
LaVece Hughes

2 c sugar
¾ c milk or cream

2 T light corn syrup
4 T cocoa

Cook ingredients in a heavy saucepan over moderate heat. Stir gently until the chocolate melts, afterward just enough to keep the fudge from burning. Cook to the softball stage until a small amount can be formed into a soft ball when dropped into a small glass of water. Remove from heat and add butter, vanilla, marshmallows without stirring:

2 T butter
1 t vanilla

optional: handful of marshmallows
¾ c chopped pecans

Let stand until almost cold. Beat with mixer until fudge is no longer glossy and is thick and creamy. Add nuts. Pour into a slightly buttered pan about 8 x 14. Makes 1½ pounds

Microwave Fudge
LaVece Hughes

1 lb box powdered sugar
½ c cocoa
¼ t salt
¼ c milk

1 T vanilla
1 stick margarine
½ c chopped pecans

Place all ingredients except nuts in a mixing bowl. Microwave on high for 2 minutes. Beat with mixer until smooth. Add nuts. Pour into a buttered dish. Can be placed in the freezer, if you are in a hurry.

"Not as good a Fannie Farmer's Fudge, but if you need a chocolate fix in a hurry, this is it."— lgh

Microwave Fudge... super easy, and good
Ann Garrity

1 tub of frosting
1 c of nuts

12 oz chocolate chips

Melt chocolate chips and frosting in microwave for 2 minutes. Stir until melted, add nuts and pour into a greased pie pan. May cool in refrigerator to harden.

Pecan Christmas Candy
Willett Saunders from Alice

1 c pecans coarsely chopped
1 T butter
¼ t cream of tartar
2 c dark brown sugar

1 c cream
2 t vanilla
1 c sugar
⅛ t salt

Place sugar, butter, vanilla, salt and liquids in a saucepan. Boil while stirring constantly until it forms a soft ball when dropped in ice water. Have greased platter ready. Add the nuts to the candy and the cream of tarter and beat hard until the mixture becomes stiff and creamy. Drop from a tablespoon into cakes on top of the greased platter or waxed paper. Should the mixture harden too quickly, pour into the platter and cut into squares when cool. Wrap each piece separately in wax paper. Will keep for a long time.

Willett got this recipe in 1938 from the Courier Journal. It came from a little African-American lady named Alice who lived in the Deep South and sold this candy on the streets. Willett thought it was the best candy she ever had— similar to pralines, but smooth and creamy rather than granular."
— lgh

Peanut Butter Fudge... Wonderful
Jean Begley

2 c sugar
⅔ c evaporated milk
¼ c margarine

¾ c marshmallow cream
¾ c peanut butter

Boil sugar and milk to softball stage. (230 degrees). Remove from heat and add rest of ingredients. Mix and pour into an 8-9 inch buttered pan.

As teachers and parents we must accept students and children as they are, while helping them to move to where they need to be.
— Shaun Reeves

Pralines ... an old Southern Favorite
Selma Dickinson

1½ c brown sugar
1½ c white sugar
2 c whole pecan halves

1 T butter
1 c water
1 t vinegar

Combine sugars, water and vinegar. Cook to softball stage. Add butter and nuts. Remove from heat. Immediately beat until mixture thickens and become cloudy. Quickly drop by heaping tablespoons onto buttered wax paper. Makes 14.

Tiger Butter Candy
LaVece Hughes

1 lb white chocolate
½ c peanut butter

6 oz chocolate chips

Melt white chocolate in a 2 qt microwave dish for 5 to 8 minutes on 50% power, stirring every 2 minutes. Stir in peanut butter and spread mixture on waxed paper on a cookie sheet. Immediately melt chocolate chips in a microwave on 50% power for 3-5 minutes. Drizzle over peanut butter layer. With knife or spatula, swirl mixture. Break or cut into pieces.

This is a quick candy to add to the variety of my Christmas candies. — lgh

Strawberry Divinity
Kate Ganter

3 c sugar
¾ cup white corn syrup
¾ c water

2 egg white (⅓ c) at room temperature
1 small pkg strawberry Jell-O
1 c chopped pecans

Combine sugar, corn syrup and water in saucepan. Bring to boil, stirring constantly to dissolve all sugar. Remove remaining sugar crystals from sides of pan with a damp cloth. Cook to hard boil stage or 252 degrees. Remove from heat and let stand for a few moments while you prepare egg whites. Place egg whites in large bowl and beat until foamy. Add Jell-O and beat until mixture forms soft peaks. Pour hot syrup in a fine, steady stream while beating constantly. Continue beating until candy loses its gloss and will hold shape. Fold in pecans and pour into buttered 9"square pan. Cut into squares when cool.

Potato Candy . . . a family favorite
LaVece Hughes from Betty Hughes

Cook one medium potato in skin, microwave for 5-7 minutes until soft. Peel and mash in a bowl with a fork. Add powdered sugar until dough like consistency is reached. (About a box) Roll out on waxed paper dusted with more powdered sugar to about ¼ inch thickness. Spread peanut butter on top of "dough" and roll up, jelly roll fashion. Slice.

"Very easy and can be made away from the kitchen at church or school with children." — lgh

White Fudge
Charlie G. Hughes, Sr. from Nettie Coy Hughes

6 c sugar
3 c milk
½ t salt

1 stick butter
2 t vanilla
½ c dates
1 c chopped pecans

Combine sugar, milk and salt, and heat until the soft-ball stage. (Forms a soft ball when dropped into cup of water.) Remove from heat and add butter and vanilla. Cool until 110 degrees or cool enough to handle. *Watch TV for an hour or so.* Beat with a mixer until begins to loose its gloss. Add nuts and dates. Continue to beat by hand until thickened. Pour into a buttered pan 9 x 12 dish.

Date-Nut Fudge
Charlie G Hughes, Sr.

3 cups sugar
1/8 t salt
1 t vanilla
½ cup chopped nuts

1½ cup milk
¼ cup butter
1 box dates, chopped

Boil everything except butter until a soft boil. Add butter, beat until ready to spread. Add dates and nuts. Pour into butter dish and cool.